The First-Year Experience Monograph Series No. 55

Students in Transition:
Research and Practice in Career Development

Paul A. Gore, Jr. and Louisa P. Carter, Editors

National Resource Center for
The First-Year Experience®
& Students in Transition
UNIVERSITY OF SOUTH CAROLINA
2011

Cite as:

Gore, P. A., Jr., & Carter, L. P. (Eds.). (2011). *Students in transition: Research and practice in career development* (Monograph No. 55). Columbia, SC: University of South Carolina, National Resource Center for The First-Year Experience and Students in Transition.

Sample chapter citation:

Pickett, R. F. (2011). Action research: The art and science of establishing real-world evidence. In P. A. Gore, Jr. & L. P. Carter (Eds.), *Students in transition: Research and practice in career development* (Monograph No. 55, pp. 17-25). Columbia, SC: University of South Carolina, National Resource Center for The First-Year Experience and Students in Transition.

Copyright © 2011 University of South Carolina. All rights reserved. No part of this work may be reproduced or copied in any form, by any means, without written permission of the University of South Carolina.

ISBN 978-1-889-27173-6

The First-Year Experience® is a service mark of the University of South Carolina. A license may be granted upon written request to use the term "The First-Year Experience." This license is not transferable without written approval of the University of South Carolina.

Production Staff for the National Resource Center:
Project Manager   Toni Vakos, Editor
Project Editors   Tracy L. Skipper, Assistant Director for Publications
                       Dottie Weigel, Editor
Design and Production Shana Bertetto, Graphic Artist

Additional copies of this monograph may be obtained from the National Resource Center for The First-Year Experience and Students in Transition, University of South Carolina, 1728 College Street, Columbia, SC 29208. Telephone (803) 777-6229. Fax (803) 777-4699.

Library of Congress Cataloging-in-Publication Data

Students in transition : research and practice in career development / by Paul A. Gore, Jr. and Louisa P. Carter, editors.
    p. cm.
 Includes bibliographical references.
 ISBN 978-1-889-27173-6
 1. Career education--United States--Case studies. 2. Career development--United States--Case studies. 3. School-to-work transition--United States--Case studies. I. Gore, Paul A. II. Carter, Louisa P.
 LC1037.5.S86 2011
 370.11'3--dc22
                         2010049602

TABLE OF CONTENTS

FOREWORD v
Jennifer R. Keup

NOTES FROM THE EDITORS ix
Paul A. Gore, Jr. and Louisa P. Carter

SECTION I: RESEARCH, METHODS, AND MEASURES

CHAPTER 1: Career Interventions: What Works, Why, and Other
Important Issues 3
Paul A. Gore, Jr.

CHAPTER 2: Action Research: The Art and Science of Establishing
Real-World Evidence 17
Rachel F. Pickett

CHAPTER 3: Quantitative Analysis of Action Research Programs 27
Briana K. Keller

CHAPTER 4: Qualitative Methods for Assessing Career Development Outcomes 45
Louisa P. Carter

CHAPTER 5: Career Development Outcomes: Variables and Instruments
Across the College Experience 55
Wade C. Leuwerke and Bengü Ergüner-Tekinalp

SECTION II: CAREER PROGRAMS IN THE EARLY COLLEGE YEARS

SAINT LOUIS UNIVERSITY
Transitioning Students From High School to College: A Career Development
Approach for Deciding Students 71

NORTH CAROLINA STATE
First Year College: A Major/Career Decision-Making Model for
Undecided Students.. 77

CUYAMACA COMMUNITY COLLEGE
Career Development in a College Success Course 83

FLORIDA STATE UNIVERSITY
Career Information-Seeking Behavior: Rediscovering an Effective
Career Intervention 89

ENDICOTT COLLEGE
Charting a Career Path: The Impact of Required First-Year Internships...................... 97

GETTYSBURG COLLEGE
A Modern-Day Apprenticeship Program 103

ELON UNIVERSITY
Charting Your Journey: Life Entrepreneurs Program................................... 109

UNIVERSITY OF RICHMOND
Destination Unknown: Sophomore Students in Transition............................117

SECTION III: CAREER PROGRAMS IN THE LATER COLLEGE YEARS

UNIVERSITY OF UTAH
A Collaborative Approach to Helping Humanities Students Find Career Success 127

THE OHIO STATE UNIVERSITY
Interdisciplinary Career Preparation: Professional Pathways Seminars........................ 133

THE OHIO STATE UNIVERSITY
Qualified Undergraduate Interview Candidate: Transitioning to
Professional Interviews.. 139

SOUTHERN ILLINOIS UNIVERSITY CARBONDALE
Assessing Career Development Outcomes in a Large Academic Department..............151

ABOUT THE CHAPTER AUTHORS 159

Foreword

Jennifer R. Keup

From our earliest years, the issue of a career pathway has been highlighted as significant. Children are often asked, "What do you want to be when you grow up?" and are invited to bring their parents and family members to participate in Career Day presentations in elementary school. High school students frequently consider their career aspirations in the selection of colleges they apply to. College students grapple with major selection as a precursor to their professional pursuits, and the higher education institutions that serve them are often barraged with requests for accountability and return on investment with respect to the employability of their graduates. National employment statistics indicate that adults change jobs approximately 10 times in their lifetimes (Bureau of Labor Statistics, 2010), a number that may very well increase as the economy changes and new professional pathways are revealed.

Clearly, the preparation and pursuit of a career trajectory is a lifelong endeavor. However, these same career milestones also suggest that our professional pursuits are far greater than just a return on an educational investment or a way to earning a living. In many ways, the search for a job, selection of a career, and establishment of a profession are fundamental to our personal sense of purpose, the development and maintenance of our identity, and even our efforts to make a contribution and leave a legacy. Often this process of introspection, interests, skill development, and occupational inquiry coalesces during an individual's undergraduate years in college. Thus, career exploration, maturation, and selection represent pivotal developmental thresholds in higher education and fundamental components of the mission of the National Resource Center for The First-Year Experience and Students in Transition to "support and advance efforts to improve student learning and transitions into and through higher education." Given the prominent role and importance of career development in the undergraduate experience and to the mission of the National Resource Center, we are pleased to share this new monograph on the research and practice of career development for students in transition.

This book is significantly updated in background, content, and format since the previous volume in the Center's monograph series on this topic, which was published in 2005. The current monograph summarizes classic and current research on career development as well as features prominent and emerging tools to facilitate this process, such as reflection, written exercises, assessment and feedback methods, individualized inventories, web-based programs, seminars (e.g., first-year, themed, capstone), advisement models, and information gathering strategies. Further, this volume identifies and encourages advocates for effective career development for college students in all segments of the institutional structure and at all levels of the educational pipeline, including academic advisors, first-year experience professionals, career center staff, faculty, alumni, peers, parents, and others who strive to provide a support network for undergraduates in their pursuit of professional direction. Finally, the editors and contributors of this volume have constructed its content around two organizing frameworks—a focus on action research and profiles of assessed institutional initiatives—that enhance the usefulness of the information contained herein and advance the intellectual and practical discussion on career development of college students.

First, *Students in Transition: Research and Practice in Career Development* moves beyond the format of the previous volume on career development in its focused exploration of career development through the methodological lens of action research. As indicated by Pickett in chapter 2 of this book, "action research can be seen as a tool to improve aspects of the educational system, enhance student success, evaluate instructor needs, and increase understanding of practice" (p. 17). At its foundation, action research is an inclusive, collaborative, transformative, contextual, empowering, and, most importantly, applied means of conducting analyses in higher education. It has its roots in activism and represents a bottom-up approach to advancing knowledge and creating change within an institutional environment. Similarly, the first-year experience and students in transition movement has its own historical roots in activism and represents a transformative movement within higher education. When coupled with the fact that the National Resource Center identifies the connection between research and practice as one of its core commitments, it is not surprising that action research resonates with the editors and contributors of this monograph as well as the Center staff who helped in its development and production. As such, we are pleased to offer a text that introduces this methodological lens, explains its use and utility for research in higher education and student transitions, and frames the discussion of career development for this volume. We are confident that the readership of this book will gain value as both a consumer and contributor of research in career development, student transitions, and higher education from a greater understanding of action research and encourage you to incorporate its principles and methods into your study of college student development, transition, and success.

Second, the bulk of this book is comprised of case studies of institutional efforts to facilitate and foster career development of college students. Reminiscent of the *Exploring the Evidence* series published by the National Resource Center, these examples of assessed institutional initiatives offer a unique opportunity to learn from one another in our field. The Center has always prided itself on being the broker of partnerships and collaborative learning in higher education, which is reflected in our proposal-driven conferences, opportunities for our network to contribute to our publication venues, service as a clearinghouse for scholarly and practitioner information, and the collaborative means that we use to advance our original research agenda. This publication and the institutional case studies it contains represent yet another opportunity for the Center to create networks of learning in our field and to showcase and connect the expertise of professionals dedicated to the success of students in transition. Additionally, the reliance of these case studies upon quality assessment methods and conclusions based upon empirical evidence helps the field of career services move beyond just citing common practices to beginning to identify truly best practices. We are grateful to the contributors and the editors for soliciting and selecting these important examples of inquiry and success in our field to advance our understanding of effective strategies and important outcomes of career development in college. We encourage readers to review these profiles of institutional initiatives and gather lessons about process, draw programmatic aspects that are transferable to the institutional context and issues you face, and challenge and inspire your thinking about the means and methods you use to enhance the development and experience of your students.

As with any publication of this magnitude, there are numerous individuals who worked to produce the final product. I am grateful to each author who dedicated the time, energy, and expertise to the success of this publication, to Paul A. Gore and Laura Phinney Carter for serving as editors for this project, and to Toni Vakos at the National Resource Center for her management of the publication process. I am confident that you will enjoy and benefit from this valuable resource,

Students in Transition: Research and Practice in Career Development, and use the content contained herein to help shape the next era of research, policy, and practice on college student career development. Finally, I am glad to have you, the reader, among the membership of this community of practice and look forward to our continued dialogue on this topic.

Jennifer R. Keup
Director
National Resource Center for The First-Year Experience and Students in Transition
University of South Carolina

References

Bureau of Labor Statistics. (2010). *Number of jobs held, labor market activity, and earnings growth among the youngest baby boomers: Results from a longitudinal survey.* Washington, DC: U.S. Department of Labor. Retrieved from http://www.bls.gov/news.release/pdf/nlsoy.pdf

Notes From the Editors

Paul A. Gore, Jr. and Louisa P. Carter

It is rare to find examples in the professional literature describing the development, characteristics, aspirations, or expectations of college students that ignore issues of career development. Leading authors, such as Pascarella and Terenzini (2005), Astin (1993), and Tinto (1987), acknowledge that career development is a critical developmental hurdle inherent in the postsecondary experience of most students. Recent volumes focusing on academic advising (Gordon, Habley, Grites, & Associates, 2008), sophomore students (Hunter et al., 2010), student success (Kuh, Kinzie, Schuh, Whitt, & Associates, 2005), and institutional excellence (Barefoot et al., 2005) acknowledge the role of career development or career counseling and advising services in promoting the successful transition, performance, and persistence of college students.

Yet, a recent report by Pryor, Hurtado, Saenz, Santos, and Korn (2007) is illuminating and may help shed some light on why we need to focus more on the role of career development in higher education. Pryor and his colleagues state that an increasing number of college students report attending college to get a better job or improve their financial status. According to Goyette (2008) this might be due in part to the changing educational backgrounds of students' parents and/or the changing educational requirements of students' expected occupations. The educational and occupational aspirations of students are at an all time high (Schneider & Stevenson, 1999), and educational attainment is unequivocally related to lifetime earning potential and occupational status (Baum & Ma, 2007; Day & Newburger, 2002). Vincent-Lancrin (2008), among others (e.g., Keup & Kinzie, 2007), describes the changing demographic landscape of colleges and universities in the United States and abroad. As postsecondary institutions enroll more first-generation students, students of color, international students, and students who are returning to college from the workforce, they are likely to encounter expectations for more responsive and diverse career development services and programs.

In Gore's (2005) earlier monograph on career development, *Facilitating the Career Development of Students in Transition*, he suggests that efforts to promote the career growth and development of college students need to be extended beyond the walls of career counseling and placement centers. In this volume, the authors explore the landscape of career education and advising programs and describe initiatives to support and encourage the career development of a range of students in diverse settings. The chapters and case studies are designed to encourage educators and student service professionals to attend to issues of career education and development in whatever context they find themselves interacting with students.

The monograph was born from the realization that insufficient evidence supporting the effectiveness of the range of programs and services designed to promote college student career development exists. At the same time, student support professionals and educators are increasingly called upon to document the outcomes of their services, programs, and courses. This volume responds to these twin challenges facing career education and development programs in postsecondary education by soliciting contributions from educators and student service professionals who could describe their career education and development programs and provide data supporting their effectiveness.

The monograph opens with a series of contributions designed to provide the reader with some context for the case studies to follow. Specifically, in section 1, Gore begins with a discussion of recent research on the efficacy of career education and career-counseling initiatives with particular emphasis on recently identified critical ingredients in career interventions. Pickett provides an overview of action-research methodologies that lend themselves to the gathering of process and outcome data in real-world settings. The chapters by Keller and Carter describe the use of quantitative and qualitative research and analytic methodologies, respectively. The first section concludes with Leuwerke and Ergüner-Tekinalp's discussion of measures that can be used to establish career development outcomes in college students.

The second and third sections represent contributions from researchers and practitioners who are actively engaged in the delivery and evaluation of career education and career development interventions. Section 2 highlights interventions that are focused on the early college years (from summer transition to college through the sophomore year), whereas, section 3 includes interventions focused on the junior and senior year.

To build on the concluding remarks from the introduction to the first monograph, career education is the responsibility of everyone in the institution who is charged with facilitating learning, growth, and development among college students. Further, it is the responsibility of those offering career interventions to choose their initiatives intentionally, based on the empirical literature, and to take steps to evaluate the effectiveness of the programs they implement.

References

Astin, A. W. (1993). *What matters in college: Four critical years revisited.* San Francisco, CA: Jossey-Bass.

Baum, S., & Ma, J. (2007). *Education pays: The benefits of higher education for individuals and society.* Washington DC: The College Board.

Barefoot, B., Gardner, J., Cutright, M., Morris, L., Schroeder, C., Schwartz,...Swing, R. L. (2005). *Achieving and sustaining institutional excellence for the first year of college.* San Francisco, CA: Jossey-Bass.

Day, J. C., & Newburger, E. C. (2002). *The big payoff: Educational attainment and synthetic estimates of work-life earnings.* Washington, DC: U.S. Department of Commerce.

Gordon, V. N., Habley, W. R., Grites, T. J., & Associates (2008). *Academic advising: A comprehensive handbook* (2nd ed.). San Francisco, CA: Jossey-Bass.

Gore, P. A., Jr. (2005). Introduction. In P. A. Gore, Jr. (Ed.), *Facilitating the career development of students in transition* (Monograph No. 43, pp. 3-10). Columbia, SC: University of South Carolina, National Resource Center for The First-Year Experience and Students in Transition.

Goyette, K. A. (2008). College for some to college for all: Social background, occupational expectations, and educational expectations over time. *Social Science Research, 37,* 461-484.

Hunter, M. S., Tobolowsky, B. F., Gardner, J. N., Evenbeck, S. E., Pattengale, J. A., Schaller, M. A., Schreiner, L. A., & Associates. (2010). *Helping sophomores succeed: Understanding and improving the second-year experience.* San Francisco, CA: Jossey-Bass.

Keup, J. R., & Kinzie, J. I. (2007). A national portrait of first-year students. In M. S. Hunter, B. McCalla-Wriggins, & E. R. White (Eds.), *Academic advising: New insights for teaching and learning* (Monograph No. 46 [National Resource Center]; Monograph No. 14 [National Academic Advising Association]; pp. 19-38). Columbia, SC: University of South Carolina, National Resource Center for The First-Year Experience and Students in Transition.

Kuh, G., Kinzie, J., Schuh, J., & Whitt, E. (2005). *Student success in college: Creating conditions that matter.* San Francisco, CA: Jossey-Bass.

Pascarella, E., & Terenzini, T. (2005). *How college affects students: A third decade of research* (Vol. 2). San Francisco, CA: Jossey-Bass.

Pryor, J. H., Hurtado, S., Saenz, V. B., Santos, J. L., & Korn, W. S. (2007). *The American freshman: Forty year trends.* Los Angeles, CA: University of California – Los Angeles, Higher Education Research Institute.

Schneider, B., & Stevenson, D. (1999). *The ambitious generation: America's teenagers, motivated but directionless.* New Haven, CT: Yale University Press.

Tinto, V. (1987). *Leaving college: Rethinking the causes and cures of student attrition.* Chicago, IL: University of Chicago Press.

Vincent-Lancrin, S. (2008). T*he reversal of gender inequalities in higher education: An on-going trend. Higher education to 2030* (Vol. 1: Demography, pp 265-298). Paris, France: Organization for Economic Co-operation and Development.

Section I:

Research, Methods, and Measures

Chapter 1

Career Interventions: What Works, Why, and Other Important Issues

Paul A. Gore, Jr.

The distribution of labor has been a primary concern of human beings for millennia. The success of early civilizations was dependent on determining who was best suited to hunt, raise offspring, gather food, and lead. As civilization advanced, the range of activities required to support societies changed and expanded, as did the training necessary to ensure success in those endeavors. The industrial revolution in the United States brought massive changes to the nature of work and laid the foundations for modern-day career education and guidance. During this period, the United States experienced an influx of immigrants from Europe to urban centers on the east coast and epic migration of U.S. citizens from rural farms to growing towns and cities. The introduction of machine tools was associated with a growth in mass-production industries, such as textiles, steel, and transportation. Modern-day career guidance was born from the conditions that emerged toward the end of the industrial revolution: namely, urban poverty and child labor practices.

Frank Parsons' (1909) work at the Civic Service House in Boston is often cited as the birth of modern career guidance. In an effort to promote sound vocational decision making, Parsons proposed a model of guidance that advocated (a) knowledge of oneself (e.g., skills and interests); (b) knowledge of the world of work, including the options available based on an individual's skills; and (c) rational cognitive processes that would enable finding a fit between skills/interests and available careers.

Parsons and his colleagues in Boston and his contemporaries in other urban centers (e.g., Jesse Davis in Grand Rapids, Michigan) provided direct services to young men and women and quickly recognized the need to track the efficacy of their strategies. Davis noted,

> As for the results that have been attained by our efforts, which, after all have not been revolutionary, but evolutionary, it is difficult to say anything in the way of statistics. But we are teaching pupils to appreciate an education, and we have given aim and direction to what is done in all our departments. We are teaching the dignity of any kind of honest labor. We are raising the standard of scholarship, because we have succeeded in connecting today's duty with future occupation. ("Grand Rapids," 1912, column 2, para. 2)

Sustained efforts to document the effectiveness of career education and guidance are the topic of this introductory chapter. Rather than review the hundreds of individual studies designed to establish the benefits of career education and guidance, this chapter focuses on the results of several recent meta-analyses that document the effectiveness of career interventions, the extent to which interventions differ in their usefulness, and the components within interventions associated with the most beneficial outcomes. The chapter concludes with a discussion of why documenting the effectiveness of career interventions is as important now as it was to the early pioneers of career counseling and guidance.

Defining Career Interventions

Interventions designed to promote career development are quite varied. Historically, researchers and practitioners in the field have opted for more, rather than less, inclusive definitions. Spokane and Oliver (1983), for example, define career interventions as "any treatment or effort intended to enhance an individual's career development or to enable the person to make better career-related decisions" (p. 100). In contrast, Krumboltz (1996) describes interventions, such as career education, school-to-work initiatives, job clubs, simulations (e.g., job shadowing or internships), and counseling and psychotherapy, as being classified into two categories (developmental and preventive vs. targeted and remedial). In fact, the vagueness of career intervention definitions may be partly to blame for the lack of cohesion in the intervention outcome literature until recently. For example, making better career decisions might encompass choices related to which math electives to take in high school, college to attend, major to declare, or job offer to accept. Although recent definitions of career interventions do not explicitly include efforts to promote job search and attainment, research describing the effectiveness of programs designed to do so will be briefly reviewed in this chapter as these behaviors are of particular interest to students preparing to transition from educational to occupational environments. Moreover, because the details of specific studies and interventions are necessarily ignored in a global analysis, such as that provided in this chapter, readers are encouraged to consult the following sources for more detailed reviews of studies and intervention strategies (Jome & Phillips, 2005; Miller & Brown, 2005; Oliver & Spokane, 1988; Phillips, 1992; Swanson, 1995; Whiston & Rahardja, 2008).

The postsecondary environments where career interventions actually occur are as varied as the definitions of career intervention proffered above. Career interventions take place in, but are not limited to, campus career services and academic advising offices, faculty offices, the classroom, service-learning opportunities, and involvement in campus clubs and organizations. Programs designed to promote career and academic decision making may be included in high school college-preparatory classes, summer bridge or transition programs, campus orientation events, first-year seminars (FYS), first-year student interest groups (FIGs), job fairs, and senior capstone courses.

Career development, like any developmental process, is a lifelong undertaking. As such, interventions in postsecondary environments occur at all levels. Such efforts might include programs to facilitate the career development of first-year students (Odom, 2005); sophomores (Gore & Hunter, 2009); seniors (Imbimbo, Nina, & Stein, 2005); programs that recognize the unique needs of certain populations, such as women in math, engineering, and science fields (Fassinger & Asay, 2008); first-generation students (Ayala & Striplen, 2005); or students of color (Byars, Thomas, & Guerrant, 2005; Fouad & Bingham, 1995). Metz (in press) offers an excellent description of the range of career interventions in secondary and postsecondary environments.

Given the developmental nature of career interventions and the array of target populations and concerns, it is not surprising that career interventions are delivered in many forms (e.g., self-help books, structured and unstructured groups and workshops, classroom experiences, individual counseling, computer-assisted career guidance). Other interventions are designed to promote specific aspects or stages of career development. For example, interventions have been designed to promote career decision-making self-efficacy, increase career information-gathering behavior, help students narrow their options, and enhance students' awareness of their interests and work values. Hildenbrand and Gore (2005) conducted a study of first-year seminar instructors and directors to determine what career development constructs were being addressed in seminars and how those constructs were managed. Further research is needed to more fully understand how career interventions are being delivered and what the foci of those interventions are on college and university campuses.

Do Career Inventions Work?

One of the biggest challenges faced by scientific disciplines, including vocational psychology and career counseling, is that of synthesizing and summarizing a large number of individual studies in order to draw valid inferences about the overall state of the field. Research studies on the effectiveness of career interventions have been accumulating now for approximately 100 years. As previously suggested, these interventions have varied in delivery modality, target population, developmental focus, and the instruments used to assess outcomes. Summarizing this literature is a daunting task. Until approximately three decades ago, investigators relied on less systematic approaches to research synthesis, such as narrative reviews. Early quantitative approaches categorized studies according to whether statistically significant effects were detected between individuals receiving career guidance and those who did not. Dissatisfied with narrative and vote-counting methods of synthesizing research, Glass and his colleagues (Smith & Glass, 1977) and others (e.g., Hedges & Olkin, 1985) turned to a procedure now referred to as meta-analysis.

Meta-analysis is a term used to describe a set of research and statistical procedures that provide a relatively objective and quantitative summary of a large number of individual findings. One use of meta-analysis is to determine whether there is a significant benefit to a set of interventions in a body of research studying those actions. As such, meta-analysis may be used to establish whether career interventions are helpful or if one type is more effective than another. An advantage of meta-analysis is that it allows researchers to draw conclusions about the effectiveness of interventions when different measures are used to assess a similar outcome. Thus, if researchers 1, 2, and 3 each used a unique assessment of career maturity in their intervention studies, meta-analysis could still be used to average the effects of these studies to determine whether the strategies promote career maturity. Meta-analysis also allows investigators to weigh the extent to which individual studies contribute to the overall conclusion. Studies having larger sample sizes, using more reliable measures, or appearing in more competitive journals may receive greater weight in the calculations of effect compared to studies of lesser quality. Readers interested in further discussions of meta-analysis are encouraged to consult Gore and Minami (2008) for a review of meta-analytic procedures and their use in career guidance and vocational psychology.

Four meta-analyses have been conducted that compared career interventions to no-treatment control conditions (Brown & Ryan Krane, 2000; Oliver & Spokane, 1988; Spokane & Oliver, 1983; Whiston, Sexton, & Lasoff, 1998). The results reported in these meta-analyses provide overwhelming support for the effectiveness of career interventions. Moreover, the beneficial effects of career interventions appear to be present in many different populations and when delivered using a variety of strategies.

Overall Magnitude of the Effect

The meta-analyses cited above compared untreated control participants to those receiving some form of career intervention. Effect size estimates from these studies ranged from approximately .30 to .44. Such effect sizes are considered small to moderate but are comparable to those obtained in psychotherapy outcome studies. It can be confidently concluded from these findings that career interventions work and that the average career client or student benefit is likely to exceed 62% of the control group clients on a wide range of career-related outcomes.

Effect Differences Based on Outcomes

The majority of published studies focus on initial stages of career development (e.g., choice certainty, decidedness, satisfaction with choice, vocational identity). Whiston et al. (1998), for example, found that almost half of all studies published between 1983 and 1995 focused on career maturity or career choice certainty or satisfaction. The results of meta-analysis, however, suggest that larger effects are observed when measures of career maturity or vocational identity are employed compared to studies that used measures of certainty or satisfaction with career choice. Considering these findings, Whiston and Rahardia (2008) suggest that career interventions may be most effective at promoting career outcomes that are closer in proximity to the developmental level of the participants or students involved. This has important implications for the crafting of career interventions and the measurement of career outcomes. For instance, researchers and practitioners should consider designing and implementing interventions that target developmentally appropriate tasks (e.g., college major choice for first-year and sophomore students and career choice and career entry interventions for college juniors and seniors).

Intervention Delivery Modalities

As mentioned above, career interventions are delivered using a variety of modalities (e.g., individual counseling/advising, small-group workshops, classrooms discussions and activities, self-help, computer/Internet). Several meta-analyses have explored how delivery modality relates to the effectiveness of an intervention. Findings from these analyses suggest that not all career counseling interventions are created equal. For example, self-help interventions appear to be one of the least helpful delivery methods, whereas individual career counseling appears to be one of the most effective strategies (Oliver & Spokane, 1988; Whiston et al., 1998). Computer-delivered career guidance also ranked lower in overall usefulness, but its benefit may be enhanced by including periodic but systematic involvement of a counselor or advisor (Garis & Niles, 1990). It remains to be seen what impact the widespread availability of the Internet and other advanced technologies will have on the effectiveness of career interventions (Gore & Leuwerke, 2000, 2008).

Cost-benefit ratio may also be an important factor in deciding how to structure a career intervention (Whiston, Brecheisen, & Stephens, 2003). Although individual one-on-one interventions are by far the most effective, they are also the most costly. Whiston and colleagues argue, and most practitioners recognize, that the increased costs associated with such services are not justifiable given the small to modest increases in effectiveness over lower cost strategies, such as class- or group-based interventions. Well-structured group- or classroom-based interventions yield outcomes that are only slightly less effective than individual interventions. Practitioners considering group-based interventions are encouraged to explore improving those interventions by including more of the critical ingredients described below and by imposing sufficient structure on those groups (Whiston et al., 2003).

Why Do Career Inventions Work?

With the results of several meta-analyses clearly supporting the effectiveness of career interventions, researchers turned their attention to ascertaining the specific processes underlying these effects. In essence, researchers sought to identify the elements of a career intervention that are associated with positive outcomes. Brown and Ryan Krane (2000) conducted a meta-analysis of career-choice interventions in which they coded for the elements of various intervention components. Not surprisingly, across all studies included in their analyses, they identified a large number of intervention strategies, including inventory interpretation, one-on-one feedback of assessment results, orientation to world-of-work information, decision-making anxiety reduction, goal setting, and the use of computer-assisted career guidance modules. Analyses revealed that five of these ingredients were consistently associated with the largest and most beneficial outcomes. These critical ingredients, which will be discussed in more detail below, are (a) incorporating written exercises, (b) including individualized interpretation of assessment results and feedback, (c) using current and reliable occupational information, (d) bringing in career role models, and (e) focusing attention on helping students and clients develop their support network.

Brown and Ryan Krane (2000) then looked at the individual and combined effects of these intervention strategies by analyzing the outcomes of studies that included one or more of the critical ingredients. Their results reinforced the importance of using critical ingredients and highlighted the effectiveness of combining these ingredients to obtain more beneficial outcomes. The relationship between the number of critical ingredients contained in a study and the magnitude of the outcome was virtually linear. Studies that did not employ any of the critical ingredients had an average effect size of .22 (two tenths of a standard deviation difference). Studies that incorporated one, two, or three of the critical ingredients had effect sizes of .45, .61, and .99, respectively. Put another way, a student participating in an intervention that has three critical ingredients will experience benefits greater than 85% of untreated students. The magnitude of these effects is considered moderate to very large using a commonly agreed upon system of interpreting effect sizes (Cohen, 1969). Of particular interest is the fact that no published studies included more than three critical ingredients. In a subsequent study, Brown et al. (2003) determined that the effects obtained using combinations of the critical ingredients were not realized when noncritical intervention strategies were combined together. Thus, the combined effects observed by Brown and his colleagues appear to be unique to these five critical intervention strategies.

Written Exercises

The use of written exercises is common in interventions designed to promote career choice and implementation. Strategies might include keeping a career decision-making journal or blog, writing an occupational comparison paper, or engaging in behavioral contracting using written goals. Brown et al. (2003) suggest that the most effective written exercises are those involving occupational comparisons, future planning, and goal setting. The use of written exercises such as these can provide all students with the opportunity to systematically reflect on their career development experiences, share those experiences with others as appropriate, and have a more permanent record of their career development process and outcome.

Several case studies from this monograph highlight the use of written exercises for the purpose of promoting career development. For example, humanity degree majors at the University of Utah were required to complete and submit reflection papers after every class period. Students were encouraged to identify the most useful career-related elements from the class and develop at least one action step they could take based on the knowledge or insight gained in that class period. At

Gettysburg College, students used their familiarity with electronic media to regularly post blog entries during an externship experience. These entries required students to reflect on career-related questions posted by the externship coordinator. In return, the career counselor liaison monitored posts and provided encouraging feedback or answers to specific issues as they arose. The coordinator for Endicott College's first-year internship program also stayed connected to students through an online discussion board. Internship students submitted a comprehensive final paper focusing on five key reflection areas, in addition to weekly journaling of their experience.

Individualized Interpretation and Feedback

The use of formal or informal career assessment strategies is common to many career interventions. For example, Hildenbrand and Gore (2005) reported that assessment and discussion of career-related interests were the most frequently included career development elements in first-year seminars. Additional assessment may also be conducted to help students understand personal characteristics, work values, or skills. Assessment interpretations are designed to help students develop a sense of vocational identity—a construct that is of primary importance in leading career theories. Although group-based interpretive sessions often result in beneficial outcomes, the degree to which students understand and internalize information described in group-based career interventions is questionable (Swanson et al., 2006). Practitioners are strongly encouraged to incorporate one-on-one sessions in their group- or class-based interventions. Brown et al. (2003) noted that the studies including individualized interpretation or discussion opportunities resulted in effects that were almost three times greater than studies that did not include such strategies.

Individualized assessment interpretation and feedback is evidenced in this monograph's case studies from University of Illinois Carbondale and Cuyamaca Community College. University of Illinois Carbondale researchers systematically explored the effects of individualized interpretations of the Strong Interest Inventory with undergraduate psychology majors in an effort to promote career decision-making self-efficacy beliefs and reduce the level of perceived career decisions difficulties. Their findings echo those of Brown and his colleagues (Brown & Ryan Krane, 2000; Brown et al., 2003) and suggest that individualized interpretations of career assessment inventories are more effective than group-based interpretations. Cuyamaca's college success course used an online textbook that was customized for each student based on the results of personality inventories. Students gained a deeper understanding of their personality type through journaling assignments and then applied their enhanced self-understanding to career research, matching their personal characteristics with the job world (combining three critical elements—written exercises, individualized interpretation, and occupational information).

Obviously, individualized interpretation is not always feasible given resource and time limitations. In such cases, optional individual meetings might be offered to students who want to further explore their results with an instructor or advisor. Research is clearly called for to determine whether the effectiveness of individualized attention is a function of perceived need for such attention or a benefit to all students regardless of perceived need.

Occupational Information

The use of occupational information is widespread in the career counseling and intervention literature. As a result of the efforts of the U.S. Department of Labor, among others, students now have access to highly reliable and current sources of academic and career information (Gore & Hitch, 2005; Hitch & Gore, 2005). Encouraging students to access this information appears to be a popular strategy for instructors in first-year seminars (Hildenbrand & Gore, 2005). The importance of promoting information gathering behavior cannot be overemphasized. Recent authors have established strong positive relationships between career information gathering behavior and beneficial career outcomes (Taveira & Moreno, 2003; Werbel, 2000). As Gore and his colleagues (Gore, Bobek, Robbins, & Shayne, 2006) point out, however, few students access sources of information in a comprehensive and systematic fashion. Brown et al. (2003) recommend developing strategies that (a) require students to access sources of career information; (b) include exposure to, and training on, those sources during the individual, group, or classroom sessions; and (c) promote exploration between classes or sessions.

Providing students with opportunities to gather information about careers and college majors is routinely used in educational settings. Hildenbrand and Gore (2005) found this technique to be among the top five strategies employed by first-year seminar instructors in encouraging career development and exploration. Not surprisingly, there are numerous examples of the use of this strategy in the current monograph. The Ohio State University's professional pathways seminars represent a systematic effort to provide undergraduate students with an opportunity to explore multidisciplinary career options (e.g., nonprofit careers, careers in public affairs, social justice opportunities). Students enroll in a pathway seminar to gather information about a profession that interests them and connect that career path to a degree plan. This program also demonstrates the effective use of other critical ingredients (i.e., incorporating written exercises and modeling—bringing in outside speakers and using instructors with real-world experience).

Another example of career information gathering is described in the North Carolina State University case study. The University's comprehensive program is designed to promote effective major and career decision making and includes required activities such as participating in a college majors fair and conducting subsequent research on specific majors, taking part in cocurricular events sponsored by academic departments, and attending information sessions hosted by faculty who describe career options available for majors in their respective departments.

Modeling

Exposing students to successful role models can be an effective way of promoting career development, choice, and implementation. Most readers were probably first introduced to this process in elementary school during career day when parents were paraded before the classroom as examples of doctor, plumber, and architect. Unfortunately, the likelihood of any student in the classroom growing up to be a doctor, plumber, or architect based on that career-day experience is very small. Practitioners should think of modeling opportunities more broadly and concentrate on experiences and processes with which their students are currently struggling. For example, graduate students or upper-class peer leaders assisting in a first-year seminar can be valuable assets when discussing the anxiety associated with declaring a major, and recent college alumni can be effective and useful exemplars to seniors in a capstone course who are preparing to set up job interviews. Instructors, faculty, advisors, and staff can serve as models to students involved in the career decision-making process by sharing their decision-making struggles, successes, and failures.

Empirical exploration of the role of modeling in career interventions has been largely ignored relative to the critical ingredients described thus far. In fact, Brown and his colleagues (2003) found only five published studies that systematically explored the role of models in career choice interventions. In contrast, many well-established career intervention programs include elements that can clearly be considered modeling. For example, the Elon University case study in this monograph describes a life entrepreneurs program where a faculty representative and an upper-class peer leader assist sophomores in developing a core personal identity and reflecting on that identity as it relates to career and future. The strengths of this program appear to reside in the shared experiences and dialogue that occur among the students during a three-day retreat; the peer-to-peer mentorship, which is reinforced by weekly cohort meetings to discuss academic and personal progress towards goals; and a shared transitions course. This initiative demonstrates the use of models (i.e., peer-to-peer, peer-to-advanced peer, and student-faculty) to promote dialogue, reflection, and discussion of shared experience—all in the service of establishing a personal and professional identity and setting goals for the future. Florida State University used modeling as the basis for a video demonstration of six career information-seeking behaviors. Students in a first-year seminar were introduced to the video during a class visit to the career center to obtain information about campus career services and resources. Study findings suggest that students who watched the video engaged in and intended to continue to use more information-seeking behaviors than students who did not watch the video. The study demonstrates that video modeling can be a practical, efficient, and effective career development delivery tool to instill important information-seeking skills.

Attention to Building Support

The role of support structures in career decision making, exploration, implementation, and subsequent career adjustment cannot be overstated. Most students have access to a network of supportive individuals, including parents, professors, student support personnel, and peers. Moreover, most colleges and universities provide ample support structures to help students navigate their academic (e.g., tutoring, advising); social (e.g., student activities office, campus recreation, housing); and personal (e.g., counseling center) development. Brown and Ryan Krane (2000) recommend intervention strategies that make these networks and services explicit and that challenge students to take advantage of their support network in systematic ways.

Attention to building support has received even less empirical attention than modeling in the published literature. Brown and his colleagues (2003) note, however, that the effect sizes associated with interventions that include components that promote support for students are rather substantial (e.g., .83). Because of the relative lack of literature, Brown encourages the use of support components as adjuncts to the use of other critical ingredients—a recommendation that is reinforced by the results of recent research (Lent et al., 2001). When one conceives of supports as the contextual and personal facilitators of progress or goal attainment, it is evident, at least in practice if not in the empirical literature, that programs including this critical ingredient abound.

The Destination Unknown initiative described in the University of Richmond case study includes elements designed to promote and assess the use of campus support structures for entering sophomore students. This retreat-based program promotes the development of faculty and peer relationships and addresses the stress associated with career planning. Following the retreat, students meet regularly in a support network environment over dinner to further nourish their relationships and seek and provide support to each other in their career exploration and development. Outcome assessment of this program suggests that participating students feel considerably more connected to their peers and other faculty after the retreat and develop, over the course of the year, strong awareness and use of career development resources on campus.

Implications

The identification of these critical ingredients in career interventions has important implications for personnel involved in career development efforts on campus. Clearly, practitioners need to review the extent to which these critical ingredients are included in current programs and services. More importantly, in developing new programs and services, practitioners should strive to incorporate two or more of the critical ingredients in an effort to enhance their program's effectiveness.

Finally, program coordinators or graduate students interested in contributing to the research base in this area are strongly encouraged to publish the results of outcome studies using interventions containing a minimum of two critical ingredients.

Job Search Research

Compared to students 30 years ago, more students today report attending college to obtain a better job or higher income (Pryor, Hurtado, Saenz, Santos, & Korn, 2007). Given this observation, it should not be surprising that campuses across the country expend considerable effort to promote the employment of their recent graduates. Career service centers take the lead in this regard by coordinating on-campus employer interviews, conducting campus-wide career fairs, and offering workshops on interview strategies and etiquette and résumé development. Academic colleges and departments are also contributing through the establishment of their own academic-specific career centers (most popular in business and engineering colleges) and through the implementation of college major capstone courses, service-learning opportunities, practica, and internships.

Research investigating the effectiveness of career interventions designed to promote self-awareness, career exploration, career self-efficacy, and maturity has been paralleled by efforts aimed at understanding factors that contribute to job search efficacy. Given the increasing focus on employment as an educational outcome, it seems prudent to briefly review this literature and discuss the implications for college student personnel professionals.

Kanfer, Wanberg, and Kantrowitz (2001) recently conducted a meta-analysis of the personality and motivational antecedents of job search outcomes. They observed strong positive relationships between the levels of extroversion and conscientiousness among job seekers and job search behavior. They also found that job seekers with more confidence in their job search strategies and with higher levels of self-esteem engaged more aggressively in job search behavior. Other predictors of job search behavior included financial need, commitment to the employment process, and the availability of social support. Not surprisingly, active job search behavior, the amount of effort expended in the job search, and the number of sources of career information used have all been found to positively predict the number of job interviews and offers received (Saks, 2006; Werbel, 2000).

Saks (2005) presents a comprehensive self-regulatory model of job search predictors, behaviors, and outcomes that focuses on the role of goal setting; active job search behaviors; and proximal (e.g., interview) and distal (e.g., job satisfaction) job outcomes. Further, his model accommodates individual characteristics and situational variables, such as those identified by Kanfer and her colleagues (2001). This model has several important implications for professionals involved in helping students with job exploration and attainment. First, programs designed to promote job search readiness and behaviors should be sensitive to individual differences in job seekers that may facilitate or hinder the job search process. Characteristics such as extraversion, job search self-efficacy, and employment commitment need to be assessed and discussed with job seekers, and program elements to promote these characteristics should be developed and implemented. Saks recommends using the interview as an intermediate career-search outcome and focusing on efforts that will increase the likelihood of obtaining an interview. Educating students on the importance of sustained job search behaviors, strategies for accessing and using reliable and productive information sources, and the role of networking will yield positive results. Once an interview has been obtained, the focus then shifts to preparing students to excel in the interview. Recorded practice interviews and workshops designed to educate students on suitable dress and interview etiquette are appropriate. Finally, program elements that help students make important decisions about multiple employment offers, effectively negotiate for starting salary and benefits packages, and anticipate early career socialization challenges will serve to promote longer-term career satisfaction and fit.

The monograph contribution by Hill and her colleagues at The Ohio State University is an excellent example of a career program that focuses on school-to-work transition. This program, based on direct feedback from employment recruiters, is designed to prepare college of business students for professional employment interviews. Through a series of online modules and mock interviews, students developed skills in how to acquire knowledge about the companies with whom they were interviewing and felt better prepared to respond to interviewer questions. Feedback from recruiters suggests that this program has great potential to promote the successful employment transition of Ohio State business students.

Career Intervention Outcomes: A Call for Research

The findings summarized above clearly establish that (a) career counseling and interventions work, (b) some delivery methods work better than others, and (c) some specific strategies or techniques are more effective than others. These same findings, however, reveal holes in the extant published literature. First, few studies containing more than two or three critical ingredients currently exist in the literature. This is surprising considering the anecdotal observation (and descriptions of case studies in this monograph) that practitioners routinely create and implement career development programs that include multiple critical ingredients. Second, very little is known about which interventions work best with which students and at which development levels. For example, do first-generation college students benefit more from career exploratory interventions that include parental education and support programs than their multigenerational peers?

Career development and intervention programs are almost a universal occurrence on college and university campuses. As such, the college campus is an excellent laboratory for studying the effectiveness and specificity of interventions designed for students with different backgrounds, expectations, and developmental levels. Because campus programs must be, first and foremost, service oriented, practitioners should consider the methods and perspectives of action research as a way of simultaneously providing valuable service to students while at the same time gathering important data about the effectiveness of their program or the relations between participant characteristics (e.g., expectations, developmental level) and observed outcomes.

Accountability in higher education might be considered a second rationale for demonstrating career intervention outcomes on campus. During the last decade, as the public has become more disenchanted with declining retention and graduation rates and increasing tuition, and as employers have become more vocal about the inadequate preparation of their recent college graduate employees (Altbach, Berdahl, & Gumport, 2005), accountability has become an increasingly significant issue. In response to these pressures, institutions are, in turn, asking their subordinate units to produce data in support of their effectiveness.

Institutional offices charged with promoting career education, choice, and implementation are not immune to this movement (Gysbers, 2004; Hiebert, 1994; Niles, 2003). Gysbers offers several suggestions for dealing with calls for accountability. First, he recommends professionals adopt a positive mindset and resist the urge to interpret calls for accountability as threats. Career counselors and higher education professionals should assume that accountability is a routine and ongoing part of their work on campus and seek training in evidence-based practices and action and other research methodologies in order to prepare themselves. Second, Gysbers encourages units to align their outcomes with division or institutional goals and objectives. When proximal or distal career outcomes cannot be intuitively connected to institutional goals and objectives, career professionals need to strive to help administrators understand the inherent value of those outcomes and how they help advance the mission of the institution. Finally, Gysbers notes that concern about accountability is not enough. Postsecondary career professionals must take action by establishing a comprehensive and longitudinal program of outcome assessment.

Conclusion

Career counselors and educators have questioned (or been questioned about) the effectiveness of their work for a century. Fortunately, today there exists a growing body of literature that not only establishes the effectiveness of a broad range of career interventions, but also offers some guidance on the form and substance of the most effective interventions. This literature has important implications for individuals involved in promoting the career development and implementation of college students. Specifically, as educational administrators call for more accountability and as directors, advisors, and instructors are asked to do more with fewer resources, the careful crafting of interventions will become a necessity. Attention to the literature presented in this chapter suggests that career professionals are most likely to experience positive outcomes when providing individual one-on-one interventions or group- or classroom-based interventions that include an opportunity for individual follow-up. Career professionals can also enhance the effectiveness of existing or new programs by including one or more of the critical ingredients described herein. Trends in higher education suggest that requests for documented outcomes are increasingly the rule rather than the exception. Professionals involved in promoting the career development of their students should take the necessary steps not only to meet those requests but to model excellence in their understanding of outcomes and evidence-based practice.

References

Altbach, P. G., Berdahl, R. O., & Gumport, P. J. (Eds.). (2005). *American higher education in the twenty-first century: Social, political, and economic challenges*. Baltimore, MD: Johns Hopkins University Press.

Ayala, C., & Striplen, A. (2005). First-generation students: Understanding the implications for career development. In P. A. Gore, Jr. (Ed.), *Facilitating the career development of students in transition* (Monograph No. 43, pp. 195-204). Columbia, SC: University of South Carolina, National Resource Center for The First-Year Experience and Students in Transition.

Brown, S. D., & Ryan Krane, N. E. (2000). Four (or five) sessions and a cloud of dust: Old assumptions and new observations about career counseling. In S. D. Brown & R. W. Lent (Eds.), *Handbook of counseling psychology* (4th ed., pp. 740-766). Hoboken, NJ: John Wiley & Sons.

Brown, S. D., Ryan Krane, N. E., Brecheisen, J., Castelino, P., Budsin, I., Miller, M., & Edens, L. (2003). Critical ingredients of career choice interventions: More analyses and new hypotheses. *Journal of Vocational Behavior, 62*, 411-428.

Byars, L. F., Thomas, T., & Guerrant, B. (2005). Facilitating the career development of African American students. In P. A. Gore, Jr. (Ed.), *Facilitating the career development of students in transition* (Monograph No. 43, pp. 137-150). Columbia, SC: University of South Carolina, National Resource Center for The First Year Experience and Students in Transition.

Cohen, J. (1969). *Statistical power for the behavioral sciences* (2nd ed.). Hillsdale, NJ: Lawrence Erlbaum.

Fassinger, R. E., & Asay, P. A. (2008). Career counseling for women in science, technology, engineering, and mathematics (STEM) fields. In W. B. Walsh & M. J. Heppner (Eds.), *Handbook of career counseling for women* (pp. 427-452). Mahwah, NJ: Lawrence Erlbaum.

Fouad, N. A., & Bingham, R. P. (1995). Career counseling with racial and ethnic minorities. In W. B. Walsh & S. H. Osipow (Eds.), *Handbook of vocational psychology* (2nd ed., pp. 331-366). Mahwah, NJ: Lawrence Erlbaum.

Garis, J., & Niles, S. (1990). The separate and combined effects of SIGI and DISCOVER and a career planning course on undecided university students. *Career Development Quarterly, 38*, 261–274.

Gore, P. A., Jr., Bobek, B. L., Robbins, S. B., & Shayne, L. (2006). Computer-based career exploration: Usage patterns and a typology of users. *Journal of Career Assessment, 14*, 421-436.

Gore, P. A., Jr., & Hitch, J. L. (2005). Occupational classification and sources of occupational information. In S. D. Brown, & R. W. Lent (Eds.), *Career development and counseling: Putting theory and research to work* (pp. 382-413). Hoboken, NJ: John Wiley & Sons.

Gore, P. A., Jr., & Hunter, M. S. (2009). Promoting career success in the second year of college. In M. S. Hunter, B. F. Tobolowsky, J. N. Gardner, S. E. Evenbeck, J. A. Pattengale, M. Schaller, & L. A. Schreiner (Eds.), *Helping sophomores succeed: Understanding and improving the second year experience* (pp. 99-113). San Francisco, CA: Jossey-Bass.

Gore, P. A., Jr., & Leuwerke, W. C. (2000). Information technology for career assessment on the Internet. *Journal of Career Assessment, 8*, 3-20.

Gore, P. A., Jr., & Leuwerke, W. C. (2008). Technological advances: Implications for counseling psychology research, training, and practice. In S. D. Brown & R. W. Lent (Eds.), *Handbook of counseling psychology* (4th ed., pp. 38-53). Hoboken, NJ: John Wiley & Sons.

Gore, P. A., Jr. & Minami, T. (2008). Quantitative research synthesis: The use of meta-analysis in career guidance and vocational psychology. In J. A. Athanasou & R. Van Esbroeck (Eds.), *International handbook of career guidance* (pp. 627-641). New York, NY: Springer.

"Grand Rapids leads in vocational work." (1912, October 27). *The New York Times.* Retrieved from http://query.nytimes.com/mem/archive-free/pdf?_r=1&res=9502E4D91F3CE633 A25754C2A9669D946396D6CF

Gysbers, N. C. (2004). Comprehensive guidance and counseling programs: The evolution of accountability. *Professional School Counseling, 8*, 1-14.

Hedges, L. V., & Olkin, I. (1985). *Statistical methods for meta-analysis.* New York, NY: Academic Press.

Hiebert, B. (1994). A framework for quality control, accountability, and evaluation: Being clear about the legitimate outcomes of career counseling. *Canadian Journal of Counseling, 28*, 334-345.

Hildenbrand, M., & Gore, P. A., Jr. (2005). Career development in first-year seminars: Current practice versus best practice. In P. A. Gore, Jr. (Ed.), *Facilitating the career development of students in transition* (Monograph No. 43, pp. 45-60). Columbia, SC: University of South Carolina, National Resource Center for The First-Year Experience and Students in Transition.

Hitch, J. L., & Gore, P. A., Jr. (2005). Living in an information age: Occupational classification systems and sources of occupational information. In P. A. Gore, Jr. (Ed.), *Facilitating the career development of students in transition* (Monograph No. 43, pp. 61-86). Columbia, SC: University of South Carolina, National Resource Center for The First-Year Experience and Students in Transition.

Imbimbo, P. V., Nina, C. M., & Stein, E. D. (2005). The career development of college seniors. In P. A. Gore, Jr. (Ed.), *Facilitating the career development of students in transition* (Monograph No. 43, pp. 177-194). Columbia, SC: University of South Carolina, National Resource Center for The First-Year Experience and Students in Transition.

Jome, L. M., & Phillips, S. D. (2005). Counseling for career choice implementation. In S. D. Brown & R. W. Lent (Eds.), *Career development and counseling: Putting theory and research to work* (pp. 466-482). Hoboken, NJ: John Wiley & Sons.

Kanfer, R., Wanberg, C. R., & Kantrowitz, T. M. (2001). Job search and employment: A personality-motivational analysis and meta-analytic review. *Journal of Applied Psychology, 86,* 837-855.

Krumboltz, J. D. (1996). A learning theory of career counseling. In M. L. Savickas & W. B. Walsh (Eds.), *Handbook of career counseling theory and practice* (pp. 55-80). Palo Alto, CA: Davies Black Publishing.

Lent, R. W., Brown, S. D., Brenner, B., Chopra, S. B., Davis, T., Talleyrand, R., & Suthakaran, V. (2001). The role of contextual supports and barriers in the choice of math/science educational options: A test of social cognitive hypotheses. *Journal of Counseling Psychology, 48,* 474-483.

Metz, A. J. (in press). Postsecondary models of career development and counseling in the United States. In A. Di Fabio (Ed.), *Career counseling e bilancio di competenze: Prospecttive internazionali*. Florence, Italy: Giunti O.S. Organizzazioni Speciali. (English version available from the author by request: aj.metz@utah.edu)

Miller, M. J., & Brown, S. D. (2005). Counseling for career choice: Implications for improving interventions and working with diverse populations. In S. D. Brown & R. W. Lent (Eds.), *Career development and counseling: Putting theory and research to work* (pp. 441-465). Hoboken, NJ: John Wiley & Sons.

Niles, S. P. (2003). Career counselors confront a critical crossroad: A vision of the future. *Career Development Quarterly, 52,* 70-77.

Odom, J. E. (2005). A comprehensive program to facilitate the career development of first-year undecided students. In P. A. Gore, Jr. (Ed.), *Facilitating the career development of students in transition* (Monograph No. 43, pp. 123-136). Columbia, SC: University of South Carolina, National Resource Center for The First-Year Experience and Students in Transition.

Oliver, L. W., & Spokane, A. R. (1988). Career-intervention outcome: What contributes to client gain. *Journal of Counseling Psychology, 35,* 447-462.

Parsons, F. (1909). *Choosing a vocation*. Boston, MA: Houghton Mifflin.

Phillips, S. D. (1992). Career counseling: Choice and implementation. In S. D. Brown & R. W. Lent (Eds.), *Handbook of counseling psychology* (2nd ed., pp. 513-547). New York, NY: Wiley.

Pryor, J. H., Hurtado, S., Saenz, V. B., Santos, J. L., & Korn, W. S. (2007). *The American freshman: Forty year trends*. Los Angeles, CA: University of California - Los Angeles, Higher Education Research Institute.

Saks, A. M. (2005). Job search success: A review and integration of the predictors, behaviors, and outcomes. In S. D. Brown & R. W. Lent (Eds.), *Career development and counseling: Putting theory and research to work* (pp. 155-179). Hoboken, NJ: John Wiley & Sons.

Saks, A. M. (2006). Multiple predictors and criteria of job search success. *Journal of Vocational Behavior, 68,* 400-415.

Smith, M. L., & Glass, G. V. (1977). Meta-analysis of psychotherapy outcome studies. *American Psychologist, 32,* 752-60.

Spokane, A. R., & Oliver, L. W. (1983). Outcomes of vocational interventions. In S. H. Osipow & W. B. Walsh (Eds.), *Handbook of vocational psychology* (pp. 99-136). Hillsdale, NJ: Erlbaum.

Swanson, J. L. (1995). The process and outcome of career counseling. In W. B. Walsh & S. H. Osipow (Eds.), *Handbook of vocational psychology* (2nd ed., pp. 217-260). Mahwah, NJ: Lawrence Erlbaum.

Swanson, J. L., Gore, P. A., Jr., Leuwerke, W., D'Achiardi, C., Edwards, J. H., & Edwards, J. (2006). Accuracy in recalling interest inventory information at three time intervals. *Measurement and Evaluation in Counseling and Development, 38,* 236-246.

Taveira, M. D. C., & Moreno, M. L. R. (2003). Guidance theory and practice: The status of career exploration. *British Journal of Guidance and Counselling, 31,* 189-208.

Werbel, J. D. (2000). Relationships among career exploration, job search intensity, and job search effectiveness in graduating college students. *Journal of Vocational Behavior, 57,* 379-394.

Whiston, S. C., Brecheisen, B. K., & Stephens, J. (2003). Does treatment modality affect career counseling effectiveness? *Journal of Vocational Behavior, 62,* 390-410.

Whiston, S. C., & Rahardia, D. (2008). Vocational counseling process and outcome. In S. D. Brown & R. W. Lent (Eds.), *Handbook of counseling psychology* (4th ed., pp. 444-461). Hoboken, NJ: John Wiley & Sons.

Whiston, S. C., Sexton, T. L., & Lasoff, D. L. (1998). Career-intervention outcomes: A replication and extension of Oliver & Spokane (1988). *Journal of Counseling Psychology, 45,* 150-165.

CHAPTER 2

ACTION RESEARCH: THE ART AND SCIENCE OF ESTABLISHING REAL-WORLD EVIDENCE

Rachel F. Pickett

Action research is a methodology that lends itself well to investigating, cultivating, and maintaining change in a variety of educational settings, including colleges and universities (Noffke & Somekh, 2009). Key features of action research include its collaborative nature and grassroots characteristics. Ferrance (2000) described action research as a collective effort among colleagues aimed at exploring solutions to real-world challenges in the classroom. Koshy (2010) indicated the ultimate objective of action research is to improve educational practices. Bassey (1998) stated the purpose of action research is to understand current educational practices, evaluate those practices, and make improvements accordingly. Action research can respond to the calls for educator accountability in higher education and serve as a formative program assessment strategy.

Over the past 10 years, action research has grown in popularity and acceptance. This growth is evidenced by its attention in the literature in fields such as education and the social sciences, as well as the inception of the *Action Research* journal in 2003. Action research has many exciting applications; this chapter presents action research as a useful philosophical framework for exploring career development initiatives and provides practical examples of action research studies. It closes with a discussion of strategies for presenting findings from action research.

Introduction to Action Research

Action research can be seen as a tool to improve aspects of the educational system, enhance student success, evaluate instructor needs, and increase understanding of practices. Ferrance (2000) pointed out that action research is not about trying to figure out what is wrong or why certain things are done; rather, it is about seeking knowledge on how to improve and accomplish tasks better. In action research, instructors and student support personnel examine their own practice in order to adjust their pedagogy or programs. Instead of relying on an objective outsider to conduct the investigation, action research encourages a bottom-up approach that begins with individuals driving their own studies. Watts (1985) outlined the following assumptions of action research: (a) educators work best on issues they have identified, (b) their effectiveness is increased when encouraged to examine/assess their own work and make changes accordingly, and (c) they learn from each other as well as enhance their professional development when working collaboratively.

Noffke (1997, 2009) created an analytical framework for action research using three specific dimensions: professional, personal, and political. The professional dimension involves recognizing that action research yields a changing knowledge base for instructing as well as a new "way of knowing" (Noffke, 2009, p. 10) or understanding practice. This dimension also focuses on how action research can function as an instrument in educators' training and improvement strategies. The personal dimension highlights the ways in which action research can be used to assist educators in making personal beliefs and educational goals more congruent with their practices and actions in the classroom, student support centers, and other higher education programs. Additionally, the personal dimension plays a role in emphasizing accountability to self and others, as well as helping educators communicate to colleagues the importance of evaluating their work through self-study and reflection. Lastly, Noffke's political dimension stresses the ties action research maintains to addressing social and economic struggles in education, as well as the importance of effectively dealing with current issues through civic participation.

Themes of Action Research

Action research has four basic themes: (a) empowerment of participants, (b) collaboration through participation, (c) acquisition of knowledge, and (d) social and educational change (Ferrance, 2000). First, action research is a method that is meant to empower educators and allow them to take research and evaluation into their own hands. By being able to identify issues and concerns that directly affect their daily work, instructors feel in control of ways to influence the educational system and make positive change. In addition, instructors can pass on the empowering nature of action research to their students depending on the types of issues they choose to examine. Collaboration through participation is another essential component of action research. Since its beginnings, action research has involved the combined efforts of educators and other personnel. The process of action research is driven by individuals who directly take part in education and serve on the front lines. Acquisition of knowledge includes expanding insight into pedagogical concerns as well as increasing educators' self-understanding. Although action research may look different depending on how it is employed in various settings, the knowledge gained is always directly connected to practice. Finally, the theme of educational and social change is important in action research since individuals who engage in the process have the opportunity to make a positive change in the world through improving education.

Action Research, Outcome Assessment, and Career Development

Action research is a methodology fit for investigating, cultivating, and maintaining change as well as exploring solutions to real-world challenges. Since a primary goal of outcome assessment is to improve the quality of instruction (Falkenberg, 1996), action research strategies that focus on making change within the context of real-world settings are a natural match. By concentrating on investigating real-world settings, action research has external validity, or the ability to be generalized to practices in the field, which is important in outcome assessment. In addition, action research combines the art and science of educational evaluation by incorporating educators' intuitive knowledge in conjunction with data collection and analysis. This also enhances outcome assessment. Lastly, the collaborative characteristic of action research can make conducting outcome assessment a more manageable endeavor.

Ferrance's (2000) action research themes can also be applied to the study of career development initiatives. The participant empowerment theme is addressed in the purpose of career development initiatives, which is to encourage students to take charge of their educational plans in such a way that prepares them for the world of work after college. Collaboration among educators, students, administrators, and community members is important when examining career development initiatives as all of society has a stake in preparing individuals for productive participation in the job world. Acquisition of knowledge that can be directly applied to practice is essential to career development initiatives because it allows students to immediately benefit from research. Finally, the theme of social and educational change is clearly connected to career programming. Assisting students with career exploration can encourage social, educational, and economic possibilities that did not exist before for individuals. According to several prominent career theorists (e.g., Gottfredson, 1996; Hackett & Betz, 1981; Lent, Brown, & Hackett, 1994), individuals may rule out particular career options based on societal stereotypes and expectations. Career development strategies have the potential to empower individuals to discover unexplored vocational potential. The link between action research themes and career development initiatives is important as it achieves the larger goal of assisting career development professionals in demonstrating the importance of their work to the educational community. This is in keeping with Noffke's (1997, 2009) personal dimension of action research described above.

Using Action Research to Establish Educator Accountability

According to Teel (see Hollingsworth et al., 2009), action research referred to as "teacher research" (p. 71) specifically represents an educator's examination of his or her own practice in an effort to implement ongoing, cyclical improvements and to provide a method of accountability. Mills (2003) and Dahir and Stone (2009) also suggest that action research can be used as an effective tool to answer the calls for practitioner accountability in education. The personal dimension of Noffke's (1997, 2009) action research framework highlights the role of accountability to self and others.

Numerous investigators make the connection between action research and advocacy efforts aimed at improving the educational system to benefit all persons (e.g., Dahir & Stone, 2009; Griffiths, 2009; Noffke, 2009). Because of the empowering qualities of action research and its bottom-up approach, educators are able to feel more in control of how they are evaluated and may be more invested in accountability efforts.

Using Action Research to Establish a Program of Outcome Assessment

Ferrance (2000) outlined several types of action research used to carry out various approaches to outcome assessment. Individual instructor research typically focuses on specific classroom issues, such as student learning or effectiveness of teaching materials. Collaborative action research often addresses particular educational issues that may be present across classrooms (e.g., student engagement via participation). Institution-wide action research engages teams of educators who focus on issues of collective interest, such as student retention. Collaborative and institution-wide methods are best suited for evaluation of programs. Finally, systemwide action research is the most complex research form and incorporates teams of educators who may not regularly have collegial interactions. For example, University 101 directors from institutions across the country might work together on implementing a career development module. Using action research to assess outcomes has the potential to impact curriculum and program guidelines as well as institutional policies.

Stages of Inquiry in Action Research

Several steps are included in the action research cycle to establish a program of outcome assessment or demonstrate educator accountability. Ferrance (2000) and Mills (2000) outlined a five-stage model. The first task is to identify an area of study, selecting a research question that is meaningful and within one's capabilities of exploring. The research question should be a higher-order inquiry yielding more than a yes/no response and adding new information to the field. Conducting a review of current literature will offer useful guidance in framing the question. Crafting an appropriate research question is essential for a productive project and can prevent unnecessary frustrations throughout the process.

The second stage is data collection. Action researchers should try to use at least three sources of data to gain a fuller understanding of program outcomes and potential action steps. Examples of data collection options include interviews; journals; video/audio tapes; case studies; surveys; academic records (e.g., grades, attendance); focus groups; checklists; questionnaires; self-assessments; student work samples; and field notes. When selecting a method of data collection, it is important to ensure that the data are appropriate and will provide relevant information about the research question. A data collection method must also be selected that can be reasonably achieved and analyzed. In addition, deciding how to organize, or group, the data is critical to useful analysis.

Analysis and interpretation follow data collection as the third stage, and methods will vary depending on the research question selected as well as the type of data collected. For example, quantitative data, such as surveys and checklists, can be analyzed to examine relationships between variables (correlations) or differences among groups (t-tests). Qualitative data (e.g., journals and interviews) can be analyzed to identify themes or common elements. More thorough discussions of qualitative and quantitative data are covered in subsequent chapters of this monograph.

The fourth stage of inquiry is to determine, based on data interpretation, whether or not action needs to be taken to improve practice and better accomplish tasks. Examining the overall picture of what the results suggest coupled with another review of the literature identified in stage one will assist the researcher in deciding if further change is warranted. If the research question has been answered adequately, no further action is needed. However, if evidence suggests room for improvement, the educator should then select one important variable to alter that has the best chance of making positive change. As this new strategy is implemented, the data collection methods used in stage two are repeated.

The final stage of inquiry is reflection on, and evaluation of, the results. At this point, if changes were made, the investigator compares the outcome of the practice pre and post any changes implemented in stage four to determine whether the practice has sufficiently improved or whether more refinement is needed. According to Ferrance (2000) and Mills (2000), action research is a cyclical process that may involve several repetitions of the five phases described above.

Koshy (2010) described several real-world examples of action research projects, and this five-stage approach is illustrated in her individual instructor research case involving Lisa, a lecturer in higher education investigating strategies to improve learning outcomes and comfort levels of adult learners in a college course (pp. 13-15). In stage one, Lisa identified her research question as, "How can we improve provision for mature students joining our teacher training course?" (p. 15). Data collection was accomplished using questionnaires, surveys, interviews, existing literature, and discussions to explore the feelings and attitudes of the adult learners in her course. For stage three, a quantitative analysis was used to examine the results from the surveys and questionnaires. In addition, an outside group of professional tutors, who were not instructors in the course, analyzed interview transcripts and discussion notes using qualitative methods. Based on the team's interpretation of the data, IT tutoring sessions, student discussion groups, assignment support, and skills-sharing activities were implemented in the class. These changes were followed by a second set of adult learner interviews (i.e., stage four). Lisa and her colleagues were satisfied with the outcomes and proceeded to summarize their results during stage five. Their findings were disseminated through presentations to fellow educators on both local and national levels and in an online newsletter.

The five-stage inquiry model is one of several action research conceptual frameworks available to the investigator. Other organizational structures that may also prove useful in designing an action research project can be found in the work of Elliot (1991), Kemmis and McTaggart (2000), and O'Leary (2004).

Development of an Action Research Program: Two Practical Examples

The following two research project descriptions provide examples of collaborative action research (e.g., multiple first-year seminar instructors and the University 101 program director participating as investigators) and institution-wide action research (e.g., collaboration between advising units across campus). As noted earlier, these two types of action research are most appropriate for program evaluation. The illustrations take the reader through the development, data collection, analysis, and action implementation stages for each project.

Example One: A Career Exploration Program in a First-Year Seminar

A two-week career development initiative that focuses on exploration of interests, abilities, and values, as well as information on the world of work, is embedded in a first-year seminar. Students complete career interest, abilities, and values inventories; participate in group activities; do writing assignments; and take surveys assessing their decision-making skills.

The investigating team (i.e., seminar instructors and the program director) is interested in seeing how career exploration impacts students' decision-making progress and identifies this as the research question. Data collection incorporates inventories, writing assignments, and skills surveys. These data are collected from students as part of the career development program.

Student data are grouped based on the pre career-program, decision-making skills survey results: The high-scoring group reflects students who have made a career and/or major decision while students in the low-scoring group are undecided about their career and/or major choice. Over the course of the two-week program, qualitative data in the form of student writing assignments are collected; themes of distress and openness to exploration are analyzed as most prominent. Additionally, quantitative data are gathered consisting of the congruence between the students' measured interests and the careers and majors they are considering. A congruence score is assigned based on the compatibility of the student's career/major decision with his or her interest patterns (i.e., a higher score signifying greater congruence). An independent samples *t*-test is performed to investigate differences between the high- and low-scoring groups of students. Results indicate early deciders (i.e., high scoring) are more distressed with new information, especially if that new information conflicts with their career decisions. Data suggest individuals who did not make career/major decisions (i.e., low scoring) are more open to exploration. Results from a posttest decision-making skills survey administered after the career program, reveal that students who made career/major decisions before the program (i.e., the initial high-scoring group) demonstrate lower posttest scores indicating they are less decided than when they began. Based on the team's interpretation of the data, an intervention is implemented to assist early deciders in career exploration.

Later, during the same iteration of the seminar, the action research team introduces an activity centered on the students' results on the pre career-program survey. Those students who score high on career/major decision making participate in a group activity that focuses on the value of being open to exploring alternative career possibilities as well as ways to deal with learning new things about one's self and the world of work. Low-scoring students partake in an unrelated classroom exercise on time management. Writing assignments on the topic of major and career planning are collected from all students and analyzed for themes of distress. The high- and low-scoring groups are again compared. Data point to similar accounts of distress among both groups and a decrease in the discussion of distressing experiences from the high-scoring students. The goal of the career development program is to facilitate productive exploration and self-understanding rather than definitive career decisions; therefore, the team is satisfied with the results and decides that no further change needs to be taken at this time.

Example Two: Educational Planning and Major Selection in Academic Advising

An academic advising office implements a campuswide program for undecided students focusing on educational planning and major selection. The program includes (a) mapping out a four- to six-year sequence of semester course schedules for a variety of academic specializations, (b) investigating careers and occupations that these academic specializations prepare students for, and (c) assisting students in understanding college requirements for admittance into identified academic majors of interest.

The research question is investigating obstacles that undecided students face in the academic advising office's educational planning and major selection program. Data collection, using mixed methods, includes grade point average (GPA) collected each semester (quantitative), number of visits students have with their academic advisor (quantitative), and case studies of individual students' experiences (qualitative). The first two data strategies are already in place; the case study data will require each participating advisor to compile a case study on a current advisee.

Students are organized into two groups based on their GPA for the most recent semester: GPA of 3.0 or higher or GPA lower than 3.0. The relationship between GPA and frequency of visits with an advisor is examined by conducting a bivariate correlation. Higher GPA students meet with their advisors more often than their lower GPA peers. Individual investigators present their case studies over the course of the semester to the entire team of advisors, and the team analyzes repeating themes. Case studies on higher GPA students and lower GPA students are matched based on academic year and first-generation college student status. A prominent theme with respect to obstacles of educational planning and major selection emerges. Lower GPA students believe that they have limited or no academic options; whereas, higher GPA students see themselves as having too many options to choose just one academic pathway. Based on the team's interpretation of the data, an additional component is added to the academic advising program for undecided students.

When working with students who perceive few academic options for themselves, advisors focus on discussion of college requirements and strategies to enhance the students' chances for success during scheduled one-on-one appointments. In an effort to increase these students' interactions with the advising office, staff coordinate workshops that offer concrete guidance for students with respect to study skills, time management, and making the most of tutoring experiences. For those students who perceive too many academic options, advisors focus on discussions linking majors to careers. The goal is to assist these students in identifying which major provides them with the most flexibility and long-term career options so they feel they are not giving up too many possibilities in declaring a major. While examining the same cohort of students in the following semester, data indicate a weaker correlation between GPA and frequency of visits with academic advisors; yet, students with lower GPAs are still utilizing academic advising services at a lower rate than their counterparts. Based on additional and extended case study data from the same students' cases presented earlier, it appears that higher GPA students have been able to successfully navigate the obstacle of having too many choices. However, lower GPA students still struggle with overcoming the obstacle of perceived academic limitations. Therefore, the team decides to conduct a follow-up action research study focused on the outcome of adding supplemental workshops to the educational planning and major selection program for undecided students perceiving fewer academic options for themselves. The team will utilize GPA (i.e., below 3.0) as a means of targeting these potential students.

Presenting Results of Action Research Programs

A key component to an action research program is the dissemination of findings. The focus of the research results will depend on the audience receiving them, as well as the purpose for sharing them. For example, when sharing results with institution administrators, the goal may be to justify programs, create new policies, or request support. It will be important to emphasize the findings and suggest how those findings confirm the effectiveness or ineffectiveness of current practices. For instance, in the earlier example of an academic advising program, it would be imperative to highlight for administrators the data that point to the need for additional career development resources for those undecided students who feel they have few academic options.

When findings are imparted to departmental colleagues, the goals may be centered on enhancing practice through instruction or curriculum development. Using the example of the career development program in a first-year seminar, it may be essential to point out how students who have made early career decisions experience distress when learning about new options. Strategies for enhancing instruction may concentrate on framing career exploration in a way that allows individuals to learn new things about the self and the world of work and, in turn, see career decisions as fluid.

Finally, action research findings may be disseminated to professional peers through conference presentations and journal articles. The objective might be to share general findings of outcomes assessment, increase the knowledge base of the literature, or pass on successful practices. For instance, using the two previous action research examples, it will be important to explicitly share the research questions, methods for data collection and analysis, and results so that others can implement similar approaches. Also, it is valuable to indicate how the action research project adds to what is already known in the field either by supporting previous findings or refuting them.

Conclusion

The greatest strengths of using action research to investigate career development initiatives include (a) its collaborative nature, (b) the focus on increasing knowledge that can be directly applied to real-world practice, (c) the ability to allow educators to incorporate the art and science of their work, and (d) its capacity to encourage social and educational change.

Ferrance (2000) summarizes meaningful benefits of conducting action research. First, action research bridges the gap between academic research and practice. It allows educators to incorporate new research findings into their classrooms and permits their practice to shape current research trends. Action research provides opportunities for professional development by helping practitioners gain confidence in their work and share with others what they have learned about themselves, their students, and their colleagues. Instructors can consider issues of their own practice in a productive way that not only helps them but also their students, colleagues, and institution. In addition, action research fosters collegial interactions and can enhance outcome assessment endeavors directed at career development initiatives by pooling resources, energy, and ideas toward a common goal. Moreover, action research has the potential to impact university and program change. It can demonstrate the practical role that career development plays in the growth and success of all college students. Action research also has the potential to enrich the exchange of ideas among colleagues through networking opportunities (Little, 1981). Finally, educators who conduct action research demonstrate increased flexibility and openness in their work (Pine, 1981, as cited in Ferrance, 2000).

Action research has many exciting applications, one of which includes exploring career development initiatives. Dahir and Stone (2009) acknowledge that action research gives educators an outlet to share the work that they do so it can be seen by others in the field as an important contribution to collective educational efforts. Whiston, Brecheisen, and Stephens (2003) also emphasize the need to conduct outcomes assessment on career development initiatives to ensure their place in counseling and educational interventions. Huber and Savage (2009) echo the importance of research as a core value in informing practice. Action research is a vehicle strengthening individual practice and the field of career development as a whole.

References

Bassey, M. (1998). Action research for improving practice. In R. Halsall (Ed.), *Teacher research and school improvement: Opening doors from the inside* (pp. 93-108). Buckingham, UK: Open University Press.

Dahir, C. A., & Stone, C. B. (2009). School counselor accountability: The path to social justice and systemic change. *Journal of Counseling & Development, 87*, 12-20.

Elliot, J. (1991). *Action research for educational change.* Buckingham, UK: Open University Press.

Falkenberg, S. (1996). *Student outcome assessment.* Retrieved August 31, 2009, from Eastern Kentucky University website: http://people.eku.edu/falkenbergs/outcome.htm

Ferrance, E. (2000). *Themes in education: Action research.* Providence, RI: Brown University.

Gottfredson, L. S. (1996). Gottfredson's theory of circumscription, compromise, and self-creation. In D. Brown & Associates (Eds.), *Career choice and development* (3rd ed., pp. 179-232). San Francisco, CA: Jossey-Bass.

Griffiths, M. (2009). Action research for/as/mindful of social justice. In S. E. Noffke & B. Somekh (Eds.), *The SAGE handbook of educational action research* (pp. 85-98). Thousand Oaks, CA: Sage.

Hackett, G., & Betz, N. E. (1981). A self-efficacy approach to the career development of women. *Journal of Vocational Behavior, 18*, 326-339.

Hollingsworth, S., Cody, A., Dybdahl, M., Minarik, L. T., Davis-Smallwood, J., & Teel, K. M. (2009). Action research and the personal turn. In S. E. Noffke & B. Somekh (Eds.). *The SAGE handbook of educational action research* (pp. 62-73). Thousand Oaks, CA: Sage.

Huber, C. H., & Savage, T. A. (2009). Promoting research as a core value in master's-level counselor education. *Counselor Education & Supervision, 48*, 167-178.

Kemmis, K., & McTaggart, R. (2000). Participatory action research. In N. Denzin & Y. Lincoln (Eds.), *Handbook of qualitative research* (pp. 567-606). London, UK: Sage.

Koshy, V. (2010). *Action research for improving educational practice: A step-by-step guide* (2nd ed.). London, UK: Sage.

Lent, R. W., Brown, S. D., & Hackett, G. (1994). Toward a unifying social cognitive theory of career and academic interest, choice, and performance. *Journal of Vocational Behavior, 45*, 79-122.

Little, J. W. (1981). *School success and staff development: The role of staff development in urban desegregated schools.* Boulder, CO: Center for Action Research.

Mills, G. E. (2000). *Action research: A guide for the teacher researcher.* Upper Saddle River, NJ: Merrill/Prentice Hall.

Mills, G. E. (2003). *Action research: A guide for the teacher researcher* (2nd ed.). Upper Saddle River, NJ: Merrill/Prentice Hall.

Noffke, S. E. (1997). Professional, personal, and political dimensions of action research. *Review of Research in Education, 22*, 305-343.

Noffke, S. E. (2009). Revisiting the professional, personal, and political dimensions of action research. In S. E. Noffke & B. Somekh (Eds.), *The SAGE handbook of educational action research* (pp. 6-23). Thousand Oaks, CA: Sage.

Noffke, S. E., & Somekh, B. (Eds.). (2009). *The SAGE handbook of educational action research.* Thousand Oaks, CA: Sage.

O'Leary, Z. (2004). *The essential guide to doing research.* London, UK: Sage.

Watts, H. (1985). When teachers are researchers, teaching improves. *Journal of Staff Development, 6,* 118-127.

Whiston, S. C., Brecheisen, B. K., & Stephens, J. (2003). Does treatment modality affect career counseling effectiveness? *Journal of Vocational Behavior, 62,* 390-410.

Chapter 3

Quantitative Analysis of Action Research Programs

Briana K. Keller

While many higher education staff members may recognize that action research could help them understand their students' needs, enhance their programs, and prove their value to administrators, few of these professionals actually initiate and complete a research study. A variety of factors contribute to this, including time constraints. Perhaps the most significant factor inhibiting staff and faculty from participating in action research, however, is uncertainty about how to execute a quality research study. More specifically, practitioners often have questions about the differences between quantitative and qualitative research, the best uses of various research methodologies, and the actual process of collecting and analyzing data.

This chapter addresses several of these concerns. The first section provides an overview of the use of quantitative analyses (i.e., rationales for using quantitative procedures, research questions that are amenable to this type of analysis, and the pros and cons of quantitative studies). The next section describes the process of designing a good quantitative research study. Finally, the remaining sections offer strategies for collecting, managing, and analyzing quantitative data.

Overview of Quantitative Research

Quantitative research involves an objective systematic investigation of characteristics that can be measured with numbers (e.g., grades, service usage, reported attitudes) and, oftentimes, a study of the relationships among those characteristics. Quantitative researchers use tools, such as needs assessments, attitude surveys, and structured interviews, to collect data that can be analyzed statistically. This type of research often examines one or more predetermined hypotheses or predictions about the possible outcomes of the study.

Appropriate Research Questions

Researchers who choose quantitative approaches are usually more interested in determining how common a certain phenomenon is rather than understanding how or why that phenomenon came to be. For example, career counselors who want to know whether or not students would be interested in a panel on green careers would likely use a quantitative approach, whereas professionals who want to know the specific reasons why students would or would not be interested in the panel might choose a qualitative approach. Four types of questions are appropriate for quantitative research: (a) descriptive, (b) explanatory, (c) predictive, and (d) causal. Descriptive research addresses questions related to how often members of a specific population engage in or participate in a certain activity (e.g., How frequently do first-year students interact with the career center?) Explanatory questions (i.e., correlational questions) analyze relationships among several variables, such as how ethnic background may relate to a choice of major. Correlational questions that go one step further and try to understand whether one variable forecasts another variable are called predictive. Career practitioners might use this type of question to determine whether the number of mock interviews a student participates in predicts the number of months spent looking for a job. A causal research question examines whether a change in one variable produces a change in another variable. Career center directors might be interested in examining whether requiring seniors to attend a counseling session actually causes an increase in the percentage of students who secure employment immediately upon graduation. When seeking to understand causal relationships, researchers need to establish different treatment groups; in other words, to systematically change one of the variables to see how doing so affects other variables. Therefore, studies involving causal questions are often called experimental or intervention research and require considerable effort.

Advantages and Disadvantages

There are several advantages to using quantitative research methods. First, researchers are able to investigate a breadth of variables and see connections among the variables. Second, because quantitative studies typically use bigger samples than qualitative studies, the results can be more easily generalized to the larger population. Finally, student service providers in higher education might benefit from using quantitative approaches because administrators frequently like to see numbers, as opposed to narratives, when evaluating programs and making budgetary decisions.

Quantitative methodologies also have a few disadvantages. While they allow a researcher to study a variety of variables, they often inhibit a researcher from studying any one variable in great depth. For example, a quantitative study might reveal that students' reported confidence in their ability to find a job correlates with their major, but it would not be able to illustrate what factors contribute to their confidence, why students in certain majors feel more confident than students in other majors, or whether choice of major impacts confidence or confidence impacts choice of major. Further, most quantitative instruments force responses and people into categories that may not fit particularly well because they cannot capture important contextual details. Additionally, quantitative research typically involves larger samples, which can be difficult to obtain.

Mixed Methods

Because both quantitative and qualitative research styles have advantages, can answer questions in complementary ways, and can address different but related questions, some researchers choose to use both in a single study. For example, a career development professional might want to know the degree to which international students feel equipped to handle various aspects of the U.S. job search process and, furthermore, what ideas international students have for how the career center can better serve their needs. He or she might choose to use a quantitative approach to understand which aspects of the job search seem most stressful to international students and then a qualitative approach to learn how the career center can more effectively address the needs identified in the quantitative portion of the study.

Mixed-method approaches and measures allow researchers to test the consistency of their findings, use one type of data to help explain another type of data, and modify features of their research approach in reaction to findings from other aspects. In short, mixed-methods can enhance the quality and scope of one's study and therefore increase its generalizability. Mixed-methods studies, however, can be difficult and time consuming requiring the researcher to be fully knowledgeable about quantitative, qualitative, and mixed-methods approaches.

Designing a Research Study

When a career development professional has decided to engage in action research using quantitative methods, the first step is designing a solid research study. While it can be tempting to throw a study together because data are needed quickly, researchers who do this run the risk of problems occurring during all phases of the investigation, resulting in a waste of resources, inaccurate conclusions, or inappropriate assumptions and program recommendations. Researchers are encouraged to be systematic and thoughtful when designing their studies.

Understanding Variable Types

As previously mentioned, quantitative research involves an investigation of a variable or the association between variables. A variable is something that can differ or change (as opposed to a constant, which is a characteristic that cannot change). Variables are the heart and soul of any research study, as they are typically what piqued the investigator's interest in the first place. The most common way to classify variables in educational research is independent and dependent variables. Independent variables are also sometimes called criterion, manipulated, experimental, or treatment variables, while dependent variables are often called outcome variables. In the example examining the association between mock interview participation and the number of months it takes to secure a job, number of mock interviews would be the independent variable while number of months would be the dependent variable, because the researcher would likely be hypothesizing that the number of months it takes to find a job is dependent upon the number of completed mock interviews.

Extraneous variables, on the other hand, might impact the relationship between the independent and dependent variables under investigation and can be categorized as participant (e.g., mood, personality, values) or situational (e.g., time of day, room temperature, time constraints). When possible, researchers should try to control for the possible effects of extraneous variables. For example, if a researcher thinks students' gender might impact study results, he or she could choose to study only one gender or include it as an independent variable. Extraneous variables that cannot be controlled are potentially confounding variables and should be addressed or considered when interpreting study results.

Writing Research Questions

Once an educational researcher has identified a variable about which he or she is curious, the next step is to formulate a research question about the variable. Career development practitioners should keep several things in mind when crafting their research questions. First, research questions must be feasible, or able to be studied with available resources. Second, investigators need to make sure their questions are clear and that the variables they intend to study are easily definable. Next, research questions should be significant or important enough to spend valuable resources examining. Finally, and perhaps most importantly, research questions must be ethical, meaning that trying to answer them will not cause physical or psychological harm to those being studied.

Developing Hypotheses

Hypotheses are predictions about the possible outcomes of research studies. Many experts consider hypotheses required for quantitative research, as the presence of hypotheses can distinguish quantitative from qualitative studies. Stating research questions as hypotheses calls for a researcher to think deeply about the study and make predictions based on prior evidence or theory, which are advantages. Using hypotheses can have disadvantages as well, such as bias or inattention to important phenomenon not currently under investigation. It is important to note that many types of research conducted by career counselors will address descriptive research questions, which do not lend themselves well to hypotheses.

Investigators should aim to craft hypotheses that will lead to useful knowledge. For example, knowing that more engineering students than nonengineering students participate in a co-op program is not useful if the program is only open to engineering students. On the other hand, knowing that White engineering students are significantly more likely to participate in a co-op than non-White engineering students is useful because this knowledge can improve marketing and outreach to non-White engineering students. In addition to usefulness, researchers should consider whether they want their hypotheses to be directional or nondirectional. A directional hypothesis specifies whether a researcher thinks measurements of one variable will go up or down as a result of variations in another construct. Conversely, a nondirectional hypothesis states that a relationship will exist, but does not predict the specific direction of the relationship. Both types of hypotheses are acceptable, and a researcher's choice in this area will simply depend on whether or not he or she has sufficient background knowledge to predict a certain relationship. Directional hypothesis testing is more risky because of its specificity; therefore, results from directional hypotheses are more convincing when confirmed than results from nondirectional hypotheses.

Choosing a Sample

A sample is a group of subjects from whom information is collected, which is then statistically analyzed and interpreted in quantitative research. A population is a larger group to which a researcher hopes to apply the results. To illustrate, a career development practitioner might want to know whether students would be more interested in attending career counseling drop-in hours held in their residence halls than drop-in hours held in the career center, but surveying all 2,000 students living in the residence halls would be impossible. Therefore, the career counselor might survey a sample of 200 students and then generalize the results to the entire residential population on campus. Normally, larger samples more accurately represent the population than smaller samples, so researchers are encouraged to include as many people in their samples as can be reasonably accomplished with the time and resources available. While there are no clear guidelines for sample size, descriptive studies should usually include at least 100 students, explanatory and predictive at least 50, and causal and experimental at least 30 students per treatment group.

An important part of the research process is selecting participants; a procedure called sampling. The first step in selecting a sample is defining the target population and the accessible population. The target population might be all first-year students at large colleges in the United States, but in order to fairly generalize the results of a study to this large population, the sample would need to include first-year students at schools all over the nation, which is usually impractical. The accessible population is the population to which the researcher can actually apply his or her results, usually students at a given school. The sample and the population under investigation, as well as the method used to select the sample, should be sufficiently described when reporting study outcomes.

There are two basic types of samples: random and nonrandom. The advantage of a random sample, identified using simple, stratified, or cluster sampling methods, is that it is more representative of the larger population than a nonrandom sample. The reality, however, is that most educational studies use nonrandom sampling because it is often not feasible to select a random sample given constraints on time and resources. There are three principal nonrandom sampling techniques. In systematic sampling, all population members are somehow listed and then every nth individual (e.g., every 10th student in the university database) is selected for the sample. Convenience samples are groups of individuals who are easily accessible for inclusion in a study, such as employers who have signed up for the career fair. Though convenience samples are easy and cheap, they are not particularly representative of the population. In purposive sampling, researchers use their judgment and knowledge about a population to purposefully select a sample they think will provide the needed information. An example might be studying members of the Women in Business club because they are thought to have detailed knowledge about the difficulties experienced by women who apply to the business school. The major disadvantage of purposive sampling is that the researcher's judgment may be in error.

Ensuring Ethical Practice

Higher education professionals should be acquainted with the entity on their campus that regulates research studies, which is usually called the Institutional Review Board (IRB) or the Human Subjects Board (HSB). The IRB helps ensure that investigators uphold their fundamental responsibility to protect their subjects from discomfort, danger, and distress—both short and long term. Most studies conducted by career development practitioners are relatively simple by design, do not involve physical or psychological harm, are conducted solely for program enhancement purposes, and do not result in publications. Therefore, action research studies are often exempt from the IRB approval process. There are some exceptions, however, such as when investigators plan to purposefully manipulate a variable in order to draw cause-effect conclusions, record data that will be individually identifiable, or deceive participants. As a rule of thumb, career development practitioners should always check with the IRB regarding whether a planned study needs to be officially approved to avoid potential issues down the road.

Data Collection

Data refers to information researchers collect about their samples to answer their research questions. Educational examples include, but are not limited to, grade level, gender, GPA, number of internships, attitudes about certain types of careers, and reasons for attending graduate school. The tools researchers use to collect this information are often called instruments. Before data are collected, researchers should think carefully about where and when data collection will take place, how often data will be collected, and who will collect the data. When selecting instruments, they need to be knowledgeable about many instrumentation issues.

Instrument Basics

Researchers should choose instruments that are valid, reliable, objective, and easy to use. A tool is valid if it measures what it is supposed to measure and, hence, if data collected with it can be used to draw defensible conclusions. Reliability refers to an instrument's ability to provide consistent results if administered, for example, to the same group more than once. A third consideration is objectivity, which refers to the absence of subjective judgment on the part of the researcher. Finally, educational researchers should select instruments that are relatively easy to use—for participants to understand and for researchers to score. Other factors to consider under the usability umbrella include whether a tool is appropriate for different gender, ethnic, and cultural groups being studied; cost; and time necessary to administer the instrument. Chapter 5 provides a more detailed discussion on instrument basics.

Data can be collected in three basic ways. The first is through the use of researcher instruments, such as observations and case notes. This is more common in qualitative research than in quantitative research. The second is from the subjects themselves, which is very common in educational research and usually involves written responses or records. The use of informants constitutes the third way of collecting information (e.g., surveying the target population's parents, professors, or friends).

Researchers can use instruments that already exist or they can create their own. If a career development professional only wants to assess students' opinions about a workshop they attended, he or she could create an instrument. On the other hand, if a career counselor wanted to assess variables such as career self-efficacy, career indecision, or career interests, an already established instrument that has been shown to be valid, reliable, and objective may be a better choice. Instruments can be found in the fifth edition of *A Counselor's Guide to Career Assessment Instruments* (Whitfield, Feller, & Wood, 2009), the 18th edition of the *Mental Measurements Yearbook* (Spies, Carlson, & Geisinger, 2010), and similar resources. Additionally, a number of appropriate career development instruments are described in chapter 5.

Types of Quantitative Instruments

Subject-completed instruments are commonly used in quantitative educational studies. Below is a description of several specific subject-completed instruments that could be useful to career practitioners and other higher education staff members. Questionnaires require subjects to answer multiple-choice, true/false, matching, interpretative, short-answer, or essay questions. Career development professionals could use true/false questionnaires to assess how strongly students believe in career myths, such as the myth that employers care only about grades. Self-checklists involve subjects identifying how often they have engaged in a certain activity (e.g., looking at jobs boards, conducting informational interviews, talking to their faculty advisors about careers). Attitude scales are fairly self-explanatory: A researcher reviews a participant's responses to a series of questions and draws conclusions about the participant's underlying attitudes. A common attitude scale is the Likert scale, which requires participants to indicate their preferences on a scale, such as 1 = strongly disagree, 2 = disagree, 3 = undecided, 4 = agree, and 5 = strongly agree. Career practitioners could use attitude scales to understand students' attitudes in areas such as career fields, job search techniques, or workshop effectiveness. Achievement tests (e.g., SAT, ACT, GRE) measure an individual's knowledge or skill in a certain area and are sometimes compared to aptitude tests (e.g., intelligence tests), which are intended to measure abilities that are not taught in school and students' potential to achieve.

Career development professionals can also use unobtrusive measures to learn about students. Examples include looking up students' grade point averages in the student database, analyzing existing data about how many males and females have attended certain workshops, and examining career counselors' records for data about the most frequent presenting concern.

Scales of Measurement

Instruments provide measurements on four types of scales, or levels: (a) nominal, (b) ordinal, (c) interval, and (d) ratio. Researchers must determine what type of data they have before deciding the type of statistic to use to analyze their data. Educational researchers are most likely to have nominal, ordinal, or interval data.

Nominal data, also called categorical, simply indicate group membership or separate individuals into distinct groups based on a specific characteristic. Examples include whether students are male or female, living on campus or off, or majoring in science or humanities. Nominal data do not indicate order; therefore, membership in one group is not better or worse than membership in another group.

Ordinal data, on the other hand, are rank-ordered and individuals with the greatest amount of an attribute are generally assigned higher ranks (e.g., letter grades). A downside of ordinal data is that one cannot tell how much higher or lower a score is compared to immediately surrounding scores. To illustrate, if students in a first-year seminar are ranked according to how many college credits they earned during high school, one would not be able to tell if the student ranked second had two or 20 credits more than the student ranked third.

Interval data are obtained when the variable being studied is measured with a scale that indicates how much of the variable is present. This measurement is able to showcase how much subjects differ on a certain characteristic. An example of interval data would be scores on intelligence tests.

Ratio data, like interval data, show both order and distance. The difference is that ratio measurements have an absolute zero, whereas interval measurements do not. Length and weight are examples of ratio data.

Data Entry

After researchers collect data, the first step in the data analysis process is data entry, which should be done with patience, care, and attention to detail. Data entry errors (e.g., entering a 99 instead of 9) can drastically change the results and the inferences one draws from those results. The importance of selecting the best software program for one's study, accurately entering and labeling data, and documenting one's work cannot be overstated.

Software Programs

Most educational researchers will use a computer program to store and analyze their data and can select from a variety of software programs for this purpose. Statistical Package for the Social Sciences (SPSS) is commonly used by educational researchers because it is easy to learn, simple to navigate, capable of running most tests higher education practitioners might need, and typically available on most college campuses. The downside of SPSS is that it is unable to perform some complex analyses. Another commonly used program is Statistical Analysis Software (SAS), which allows researchers to conduct an array of complicated analyses and has stronger data management capability, but is typically a bit more difficult for beginning users to learn. In studies requiring only basic analysis (e.g., means, correlations), Microsoft Excel can also be an option.

Helpful Tips

Regardless of what program a researcher uses, it is critical that data be entered and identified correctly. Below are a few tips for entering data efficiently.

- *Data structure* — Rows generally represent participants and columns usually represent variables. In higher education, for example, each row would contain data on a different student and each column would have students' responses to a different survey question (Table 3.1).
- *Identification numbers* – Researchers should assign a unique identifier for each participant in the study (e.g., name, university ID number, university e-mail address). It is advisable to randomly assign an identification number to each student that will be used solely for the purpose of the study. For example, a career counselor conducting a study could write a unique number on each person's survey and then only enter those identification numbers

into the spreadsheet, rather than each person's name. This practice enables the counselor to share the data file with others without violating confidentiality and privacy policies.

- ◇ *Variable names* – A short name should be created for each variable in the study and columns need to be labeled accordingly. Ideal names are descriptive and intuitive. For example, one might indicate the number of internships students have done by NumIntern. Researchers are advised to record all brief variable names and their corresponding definitions for later reference.
- ◇ *Variable coding* – Many times researchers study variables that do not have a numerical value, such as gender. In these situations, each possible option should be given a different numerical value, or code, and this number is then used in data entry. For example, female could be coded as 1 and male could be coded as 2. Since arithmetic operations (i.e., addition, subtraction, averages) cannot be performed on nominal data, the assignment of numbers to nominal categories is arbitrary.
- ◇ *Missing data* – Oftentimes students accidentally skip a question or two, which results in missing data. Data from these students are still useable. Researchers should consult their statistics program manual to determine how to designate missing data. Leaving the cell blank is usually the appropriate choice.
- ◇ *Documentation* – As has already been stated, accurate documentation is very important. Forgetting what a certain numerical value or variable label means can waste time at best, and result in inaccurate research conclusions and subsequent programming recommendations at worst.

Table 3.1

Survey Scores for Males and Females in Two Course Sections

Student	Gender	Section	Learned	Satisfied	Refer
001	1	1	3	2	2
002	1	1	3	1	2
003	2	2	5	5	4
004	2	2	4	2	3
005	1	3	2	5	3
006	2	3	3	4	4

Data Management

After entering data into one of the programs described above, researchers should take a number of intermediate steps before running statistical tests on the data. Data accuracy must be reviewed. Conducting some quick descriptive statistics (e.g., mean, maximum and minimum value, frequency distribution) can provide verification there are no obvious data-entry errors. If there are true outliers (i.e., scores that fall far outside the range of scores for the majority of participants) researchers might choose to run the analysis with and without those participants and consider the implications of any differences they observe.

Another data management technique involves combing through items and forming a summary score. There are several types of summary scores. The first is a scale score. On a 20-question course evaluation survey, career counselors might realize that five of the questions essentially assess whether students feel they learned important information in the course. Rather than analyzing responses to each individual question, the instructor might choose to combine the scores on those five questions to provide a more stable measure of learning. A second type of summary score is a total score. On brief surveys that assess a specific construct, such as attitudes about networking, it often makes more sense to total the responses to all survey questions to obtain an overall score rather than individually analyze responses to each question, as analyses based on item-level data are less stable and more prone to fluctuations than total scores.

Statistical Procedures

There are a variety of statistical procedures available, which can be divided into two broad categories: descriptive and inferential. *Descriptive* statistics provide a snapshot of a specified sample at a certain point in time and are used to answer descriptive and explanatory research questions. They have two primary advantages: They are generally simple to calculate and easy for lay audiences to understand. The two main disadvantages of using descriptive statistics are they do not show how individual students differ in a statistically significant way, and they cannot be used to infer how the results from a study might generalize to a broader population.

Inferential statistics, on the other hand, provide a fundamental statistical comparison between individuals within a sample. Inferential statistics help answer predictive and causal research questions. Though not always the case, researchers would generally choose inferential statistics over descriptive statistics when they want to study a sample and then use the results to generalize, or make inferences about, the larger population from which the study sample was selected. For example, career counselors would use inferential data analytic techniques to determine whether two or more groups of students differ from one another on a certain characteristic. The outcome of an inferential statistical procedure is affected by a number of factors, such as the size of the study sample, the degree to which the study sample represents the full population under investigation, and the degree to which individuals within the sample vary on key characteristics.

Descriptive Statistical Tools

The most commonly used tools in descriptive evaluations include frequency, percentage, measures of central tendency (i.e., mean, median, and mode), measures of variability (i.e., standard deviation and range), and correlations. One often overlooked descriptive statistic is the number of students who were surveyed or participated in a program or intervention. Participant numbers and survey response rates are critical values to report as they enable the reader to judge the generalizability of the findings. When the overall number of participants differs from the number of survey or instrument responses being reported, it is essential to state both these values. Moreover, it is often helpful to express the absolute number of survey responses as well as the percentage of total respondents represented by that value. This can be accomplished very easily through the use of data tables.

Frequency and percentage. The two basic ways to describe data are frequencies and percentages. Both of these data description tools can be used on nominal, ordinal, interval, and ratio data. Frequency is simply the number of subjects or students a researcher is describing. Career development professionals might use a frequency to describe how many students rated the career planning course as *highly effective* by circling 4 on the evaluation form. In a data set where 20 rated the course as *highly effective*, this would be indicated by $f = 20$.

Percentage is the number per 100 students who scored a certain way or had a certain characteristic. Career counselors might be interested in knowing what percentage of the student body is studying within each college so they can plan programs that have the potential to reach the largest number of students. When reporting a percentage, it is helpful to also report the associated frequency so readers will know, for example, whether 12% equals 15 or 1,500 students.

Measures of central tendency. When researchers want to indicate how the typical person within a study scored on a certain measure, they often report a measure of central tendency. There are three primary measures of central tendency. Table 3.2 presents the corresponding symbols.

The most popular measure of central tendency is the *mean*. Often simply called the average, the mean is the balance point in a distribution. The mean can be calculated on interval or ratio data. For example, to gauge the interest level for a new course, students could be asked to indicate their preference on a survey question using a Likert scale. A mean score would then be calculated for all survey respondents and used to help decide whether there was sufficient interest to create the new course.

Another measure of central tendency is the *median* or the middle point in a distribution where half of the cases fall below the value and half fall above. With an odd number of scores, the median is the value that is in the middle when scores are arranged from lowest to highest. For an even number of scores, the median is calculated by summing the two middle scores and dividing by two. An advantage of the median is that it is not sensitive to extreme scores. Therefore, the median should be reported when working with interval and ratio data that include outliers. For example, if a counselor noticed that 2 of 40 workshop participants gave the lowest possible score to each of 10 workshop evaluation questions without even reading the questions, the counselor might choose to calculate the median because it would be less affected by these two outliers than the mean.

The final measure of central tendency is the *mode*, which is the score that occurs most frequently in a data set. There can be multiple modes in a distribution, which is a disadvantage of this test, and it is not frequently used in educational research. Despite its limitations, however, the mode is a good choice when working with nominal data. For instance, if a career center asked students to vote for their favorite counselor by circling 1 for Sam, 2 for Kelly, and 3 for Terry, the counselor whose number was circled the most times would be crowned the favorite.

Table 3.2

Symbols for Common Statistical Tests

ANOVA	F
Chi square	χ^2
Correlation	r
Degrees of freedom	df
Frequency	f
Mean	$M, m, \bar{x}$
Percentage	$P, \%$
Range	R
Standard deviation	S, SD
Statistical probability	p
t-test	t

Measures of variability. Variability describes the spread and dispersion of data indicating how subjects differ from one another. It is common for researchers to indicate variability in conjunction with a measure of central tendency and failing to do so can be misleading. For example, if the mean posttest score on career self-efficacy was nearly identical for students in two career-related first-year seminars, one might assume that each instructor had been equally effective in enhancing students' self-efficacy. However, a different conclusion might be drawn upon learning that the spread of scores in one class was much greater than the spread in the other group. Just as with measures of central tendency, there are different measurements of variability and their symbols are shown in Table 3.2.

The *standard deviation* is the most popular measure of variability and indicates the degree to which an individual's score differs from the mean of the group. Higher standard deviations indicate greater variability in scores; that is, more distance between the lowest and highest scores within a data set. In most normal distributions, one can assume that about two-thirds of the scores will lie within one standard deviation of the mean (i.e., one third above the mean and one third below the mean).

Another measure of variability is the *range*, which is calculated by subtracting the lowest score from the highest score. While easy to use, a disadvantage of the range is that it is based solely on the two most extreme scores and is thus highly susceptible to outlying scores. For example, in a data set that has one score of 2.2, ten scores of 33.3, and one score of 77.7, the range will indicate substantial variability (i.e., 2.2 to 77.7) while, in reality, 10 of the 12 scores were identical and not variant at all.

Correlations. The mean, median, and mode are useful tools to use when examining only one variable. A *correlation* is calculated when researchers want to see if there is a relationship between two different variables within a group of students. Correlations are used to address explanatory research questions (i.e., correlational questions), and results can be positive or negative. In a positive or direct correlation, students who score high on the first measure also score high on the second measure. In a negative or inverse relationship, students who score high on one variable score low on the other variable. Negative correlations are often just as interesting and important as positive ones. For example, if students' career engagement scores were negatively correlated with their career self-efficacy scores, further study may be warranted.

It is important to note that correlations simply show differences and similarities. They do not indicate causation, and assuming a cause and effect relationship based solely on a correlation is inappropriate. To illustrate, if the number of hours per week a student spends on homework is found to correlate positively with GPA, researchers cannot state with certainty that spending more time on homework actually causes, or results in, higher grades.

There are a variety of different correlations (r), but the most commonly used is the Pearson product-moment coefficient of correlation. The value of r ranges from -1.00 to +1.00. When r is close to zero, the relationship between the two variables is weak or nonexistent. When r is close to -1.00 or +1.00, the variables have a strong negative/inverse relationship or a strong positive/direct relationship, respectively.

Visual Representations of Descriptive Statistics

It can be helpful to showcase data collected from a study in a graph or chart. Nominal or categorical data are often presented in a frequency table, which shows the number of times each score occurred in the data set (e.g., Table 3.3 lists how many first-year students declared specific majors). Other visual representations of nominal data include bar graphs and pie charts.

Table 3.3

Declared Majors of First-Year Students

Major	Frequency
Social Science	250
Humanities	200
Engineering	150
Science	100
Art	50

Interval and ratio data are better captured in a frequency polygon or histogram. A frequency polygon (a) lists all the possible scores (or score intervals) on the horizontal axis, starting with the lowest score on the left; (b) lists the possible frequencies with which each score could have been received on the vertical axis, starting with zero at the bottom; (c) shows a dot where each score intersects with the frequency with which it occurred in the data set; and (d) shows a line connecting each dot. A sample frequency polygon depicting students' ratings of a workshop is shown in Figure 3.1.

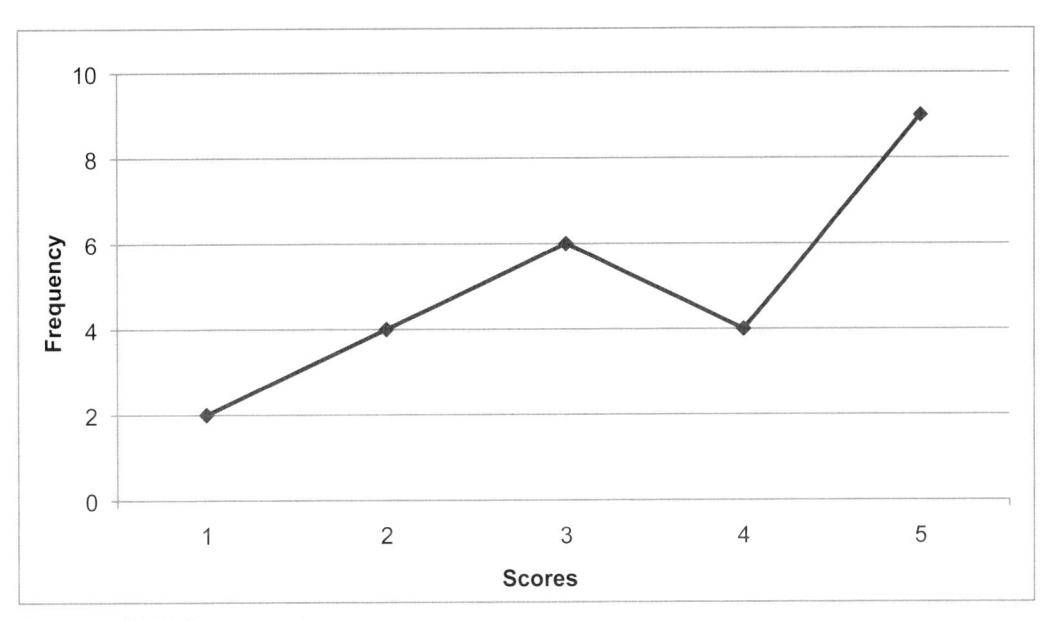

Figure 3.1. Workshop evaluation scores.

A histogram looks similar to a bar graph, however, the variables on the horizontal axis are always contiguous or consecutive intervals, whereas, bar graph variables can be contiguous or non-contiguous. The horizontal axis lists the possible scores, the vertical axis lists the possible frequencies (always starting with zero), and columns erupt from the horizontal axis to heights corresponding to the frequency each score occurred. A sample depicting students' responses to a career engagement inventory is shown in Figure 3.2.

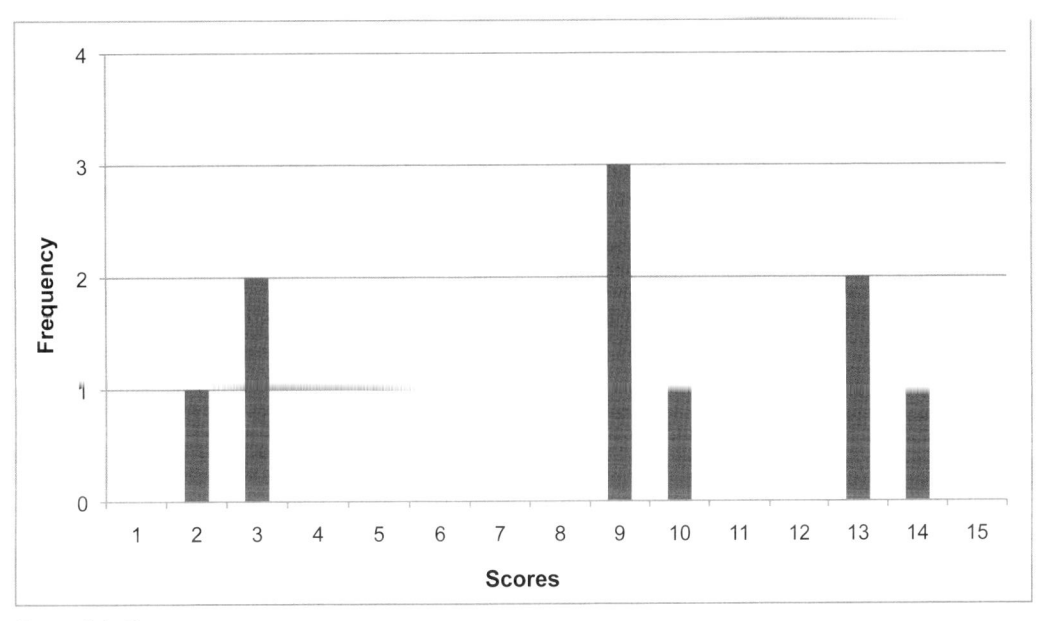

Figure 3.2. Career engagement scores.

Inferential Statistical Tools

There are several inferential techniques researchers can employ, and selection is generally based on the type of data, however, investigators must also consider additional factors, including number of groups within a sample, relationship among groups within a sample, number of independent and dependent variables, sample size, and the presence or absence of a pretest. The three most commonly used inferential techniques (i.e., *t*-test, ANOVA, and chi square) are discussed in the following sections, and the symbols associated with these three tests can be found in Table 3.2.

***t*-test.** The first inferential technique frequently used in action research is the *t*-test, which indicates whether the means of two samples are significantly different from one another. For example, a *t*-test could be used to learn whether male and female's responses to a measure of career indecision differ significantly or to investigate whether the career engagement scores for students who participated in a certain program are significantly higher than the scores of students who did not participate in the program.

There are two types of *t*-tests: (a) one for uncorrelated or independent data to compare the means of two different groups and (b) the other for correlated or dependent data to compare the mean score of a group at two different times (e.g., comparison of pre- and postintervention scores). A correlated *t*-test can also be used when conducting a study that involves two groups who are matched on a certain characteristic.

Reporting the results of a *t*-test requires several steps.

1. Record the means, standard deviations, and size of the two groups compared (typically done in a table).
2. List the actual numerical value of the *t*-test.
3. Indicate the statistical probability level (i.e., the value that indicates whether or not there is a significant relationship between the groups). The most commonly reported statistical probability levels are .05 (significant), .01 (more significant), and .001 (highly significant). Probability levels greater than .05 (e.g., .06) are not statistically significant.
4. Log the degrees of freedom for all inferential procedures to provide an indication of the size of the sample being used.

Table 3.4 illustrates the use of a *t*-test to report the differences in the results of a confidence inventory administered to students in two different sections of a course (i.e., one that included a strengths assessment and one that did not) to determine if the two groups differed in their level of confidence regarding articulating their strengths in a job interview. The results can be reported as ($t = 3.59, df = 28, p < .001$). The statistical probability level ($p < .001$) indicates that the two groups of students scored statistically significantly differently on the confidence measure. If the results of the *t*-test were not significant, the probability level would be reported as $p > .05$. It is important to note that the *t*-test itself does not indicate which group's performance was more desirable. This information is only available by inspecting the mean scores.

Table 3.4

Two-Sample t-test

	Section 101	Section 102
Mean	3.70	2.53
Variance	1.03	0.84
Observations	15	15
df	28	
t-stat	3.59	
p	0.001	

ANOVA. The *t*-test is a good statistical procedure to use when a researcher only wants to compare the means of two groups. If it is desirable to determine whether there are statistically significant differences among three or more groups, a researcher should use an ANOVA, also called an *F* test. An example might be a career counselor who wants to find out if there are statistically significant differences between students who take five different sections of a career exploration course. The results of an ANOVA are reported and interpreted much like the results of a *t*-test.

An ANOVA by itself can only show that a statistically significant difference exists, not where the difference exists. Therefore, in the previous sample scenario, a statistically significant ANOVA value would tell the career counselor that there is a difference between at least two of the course sections but would not indicate between which sections the difference was measured. To determine where exactly the significant differences lie, the career counselor would need to conduct a post hoc analysis, which is a procedure used to further delineate patterns in the data that were not fully identified in the initial statistical analysis. There are many types of post hoc analyses, based on different assumptions and used for different purposes. Two widely used post hoc tests in social sciences include the Tukey's Honestly Significant Difference (HSD) test and Scheffe's test (Shavelson, 1996).

Chi Square. The *t*-test and ANOVA are popular inferential techniques for data that are interval or ratio in nature, such as numerical scores on assessments and program evaluations. If educators want to test for statistically significant differences when working with nominal or categorical data (i.e., data that do not have mean values to compare), chi-square analyses are appropriate. Using a chi-square analysis enables researchers to examine categorical data gathered from one sample and make inferences about the population from which the sample was drawn.

For example, Table 3.5 lists the number of male and female graduating seniors who have and have not secured jobs. Looking at the data, an advisor might assume that graduating males are more successful in obtaining employment than graduating females. But, due to potential sampling errors (i.e., likely differences between the sample that was surveyed, other samples within the target population, and the entire population from which the sample was drawn), the advisor cannot necessarily assume that these frequencies would hold true for the entire population of graduating students at the university. Thus, a chi-square statistic should be calculated to see if these frequencies differ systematically from the theoretically expected frequencies of the population or are due to chance.

Table 3.5

Jobs Secured by Males and Females

	Job secured	No job secured
Males	30	20
Females	20	30

A standard chi-square test table is shown in Table 3.6. The most important pieces of information in the table are the value, degrees of freedom, and significance associated with the Pearson chi square (the top row of the table). The significance level of .045 indicates that the observed frequencies of males in females in the two conditions were significantly different from each other. The Pearson chi square value of 4.0 indicates that such an unequal distribution of males and females across the two conditions would be expected by chance only 4 times out of 100. Using the data in both tables to discern how the genders differ in their distribution suggests that males were more likely than females to have secured a job prior to graduation. The results of the chi square analysis are reported and interpreted in a similar fashion as the results of a *t*-test or ANOVA. For this example, $\chi^2 = 4.0$, $df = 1$, $p < .05$, with p indicating the result was statistically significant.

Table 3.6

Chi-Square Tests

	Value	*df*	Sig. (2-sided)
Pearson chi square	4.0	1	.045
N of valid cases	100		

Conclusion

Many higher education professionals who work in career centers, first-year program offices, and related departments are faced with an array of questions related to students' academic, personal, and career development. Oftentimes, these questions can be appropriately addressed with a quantitative research study (i.e., a systematic investigation of characteristics that can be assessed with instruments and analyzed with numbers). For example, a descriptive study could provide information about how many career possibilities first-year students are considering; an explanatory study might explore how gender and use of career services relate to one another; a predictive study would help assess whether attendance at workshops leads to enhanced job search outcomes; and a causal study could shed light as to whether one career intervention produces better outcomes than another career intervention.

This chapter has addressed how to select an appropriate methodology; plan a quality study; and collect, enter, and analyze data. The information is intended to enhance career development professionals' knowledge, sophistication, and confidence regarding the design and implementation of quantitative action research programs and to encourage professionals to initiate this research.

References and Additional Resources

Der, G., & Everitt, B. S. (2008). *A handbook of statistical analyses using SAS* (3rd ed.). Danvers, MA: CRC Press.

Fraenkel, J. R., & Wallen, N. E. (2008). *How to design and evaluate research in education* (7th ed.). New York, NY: McGraw-Hill.

Kinnear, P. R., & Gray, C. D. (2008). *SPSS 16 made simple.* East Sussex, UK: Psychology Press.

Pyrczak, F. (2006). *Making sense of statistics: A conceptual overview* (4th ed.). Glendale, CA: Pyrczak Publishing.

Salkind, N. J. (2009). *Statistics for people who (think they) hate statistics: Excel 2007 edition* (2nd ed.). Thousand Oaks, CA: Sage.

Schmuller, J. (2009). *Statistical analysis in Excel for dummies.* Hoboken, NJ: Wiley.

Shavelson, R. J. (1996). *Statistical reasoning for the behavioral sciences.* Boston, MA: Allyn & Bacon.

Spies, R. A., Carlson, J. F., & Geisinger, K. F. (Eds.). (2010). *Mental measurements yearbook* (18th ed.). Lincoln, NE: University of Nebraska Press.

Suskie, L. A. (1996). *Questionnaire survey research: What works* (2nd ed.). Tallahassee, FL: Association for Institutional Research.

Whitfield, E. A., & Feller, R.W., & Wood, C. (Eds.) (2009). *A counselor's guide to career assessment instruments* (5th ed.). Broken Arrow, OK: National Career Development Association.

Chapter 4

Qualitative Methods for Assessing Career Development Outcomes

Louisa P. Carter

Higher education professionals today must prepare their students for an increasingly complex world of work (Schultheiss, 2005; Subich, 1996). Students seeking career services today are more likely than in past decades to be first-generation college students, international in origin, fully engaged in work while attending school, and have additional family obligations. These unique experiences can create different conceptions of work. Career development professionals are constantly faced with new challenges in understanding different perspectives and providing effective service.

Career counselors and educators have long relied on the use of evaluation to inform and develop practice. Although some qualitative methods are widely used in practice (e.g., card sorts, genograms), quantitative methods, such as pre- and posttesting and career inventories, are far more common (McMahon, Patton, & Watson, 2003). Researchers and practitioners are increasingly turning their attention to qualitative career evaluation methods in order to understand the complexity of peoples' lives and how that complexity shapes career development (Blustein, Kenna, Murphy, DeVoy, & DeWine, 2005). Specifically, the collaborative nature of qualitative research uses the experiences and perspectives of both the evaluator and the participant. For example, in a narrative design study, instead of simply recording an observation objectively, the evaluator listens and helps the participant create and understand the meaning of a personal experience. Similar to the principles of action research as described earlier in this monograph, qualitative methods share the dynamic nature intended to empower career professionals by drawing on their direct experience and intuition and students by actively valuing their voices and needs in the process of creating an effective career intervention.

Qualitative Research and Assessment: An Overview

Qualitative assessment methods are more dynamic than quantitative methods, and employ more expressive means of gathering information. Professionals rely on quantitative methods generally to draw conclusions about a program outcome using numerical data and objective measures. For example, using a Likert scale, a student describes her experience by choosing a number from the range in response to the prompt, "I am confident in my college major choice." The sum of the numerical responses would create a scale score, which could then be easily compared to other students' scores, and/or be further analyzed based on relevant criteria. By contrast, a professional using qualitative methods to determine the confidence of major choice, might engage the student in a structured interview with open-ended prompts, such as "Tell me how you feel about your major choice." Instead of being limited by a predefined response, the student is able to give a more detailed and personally relevant account of his or her experience. The professional listens for themes or language that reveal fears, hopes, or unique experiences. Some advantages of this process are that it (a) provides a place for the student to talk about and process his/her experience, (b) ensures that the student feels cared for and valued, (c) establishes a relationship between student and institution, and (d) presents the professional with first-hand knowledge of how a student negotiates the major selection process.

Overview of Models

Many different models of qualitative inquiry exist, from systematic conceptualizations to less structured and more flexible frameworks. Each one is unique in its contribution to understanding the complexity of human experience. For the purposes of assisting career practitioners seeking to understand and design a qualitative study, this section will focus on qualitative models used in the field of vocational psychology and other related contexts, including grounded theory (Glaser & Strauss, 1967), consensual qualitative research (Hill, Thompson, & Williams, 1997), narrative research, and case study. An overview of each model and analysis is provided below.

Grounded Theory and Grounded Analysis

Grounded theory was developed in the 1960s as a way to generate hypotheses directly from studying participants' actions, interactions, and social processes, partly in reaction to theories that felt more removed from the context of the population being examined (Creswell, 2007; Strauss & Corbin, 1998). Similar to action research, grounded theory takes advantage of the direct knowledge available from both the instructors and participants in a given setting. By studying all forms of data, the career practitioner develops a theory that might help explain the process or provide a framework for future research in the context of the institutional setting.

Creating a theory involves gathering data, finding major themes within the data, and determining how these themes relate to one another. Collected data can take many forms, typically 20-30 interviews paired with relevant observations and documents, all of which represent the question posed or concern under study. For example, in the case study from Elon University, qualitative grounded theory is used to evaluate the impact of their Life Entrepreneurs Program on sophomores' development as young adults and future professionals. Specifically, the University was interested in how these students integrated personal meaning with their experience in the program. Data collection included two initial interviews; the first consisted of open-ended questions to establish rapport, elicit students' reasons for signing up, and gain the participants' sense of themselves. In conjunction with the interview, the students were asked to incorporate a map of core identity they had made during the program. A second follow-up interview focused on the students' direct experience in the Life Entrepreneurs Program and how it would influence their future plans in college and in life. To analyze the data, the interviews were transcribed and coded for statements that reflected the meaning that each student attached to their experiences. This first step is called *open coding*, when the researcher identifies the major categories of information. A *category* is a unit of information in the form of events, happenings, or instances (Strauss & Corbin, 1990). Another way to think about creating categories is to try to identify what is happening in the text by seeking out the common nouns, adjectives, and adverbs and asking, "What is this about? What is being referenced here?" For example, such categories could be information gathering, friendship, teacher-student relationships, and anxiety. The second phase is referred to as *axial coding*, where the researcher identifies one major category on which to focus, and subsequently creates categories around this core phenomenon with the existing data. At Elon, after the practitioners found initial themes, they re-examined the raw interview data, guided by the new interpretations from the first phase.

The final results for this study provided Elon with information about the meaning their students made. Specifically, this study concluded that students showed a growing ability to construct their own identity by intentionally integrating their own desires with reasonable demands of school.

Data refinements can be added between the first and second stages, such as determining the type of category: *causal* (Did this category influence action?), *strategic* (Does this category represent actions in response to core phenomenon?), *intervening* (Did this category occur between two events?), or *consequences* (Was this category the result of an action?). The third phase is called *selective coding*, when the researcher assembles a story that best represents how the categories relate with each other in the model. The final phase, *theory articulation*, happens at the end of the study, and the researcher can express theories about the phenomenon under study in the form of either a narrative statement, a visual picture, or a series of hypotheses or propositions (Creswell, 2007).

Grounded theory is particularly useful if one has close access to a specific population about which limited information exists. For example, theories generated from traditional-aged students are likely to be inadequate in describing the experiences of nontraditional students. A grounded theory approach will be useful in examining nontraditional students' navigation of the university system and future job market, applying qualitative methods may be beneficial for developing new perspectives of how these students move through this process, since. Once established, grounded theories can be validated or tested through quantitative methods.

Consensual Qualitative Research (CQR)

CQR was developed in the late 1990s as a response to a perceived ambiguity of how to conduct qualitative research and assessment (Hill et al., 1997). By integrating various features from existing methods, mostly from grounded theory, the goal for establishing CQR was to create a mode of assessment that was always rigorous and easy to learn (Hill et al., 2005). The main purpose is to study narrative data and develop hypotheses and theories by analyzing themes.

There are several key features of CQR. The first is using the consensus of multiple people (e.g., fellow career practitioners) to uncover and construct themes and meaning from the data. This method may be useful in an institutional setting because it allows the input of multiple persons, adding many perspectives to the analysis. CQR, like grounded theory, seeks the value of the words and direct experience provided from naturalistic settings. However, it differs by providing more structure in the interview process to accurately represent the participant's experience with less influence from the researchers (Hill et al., 2005). For example, if a career counseling center wanted to evaluate which components of their counseling process were more useful to their students, using CQR, all of the counselors might meet to discuss concerns and to brainstorm a set of questions to ask students at the end of a session. Every counselor would follow through with the same protocol for each student. The counselors would reconvene to analyze the data. CQR has been used most frequently in the field of career development in studies that aim to understand the world of work from understudied subjective perspectives (Blustein et al., 2005).

CQR data analysis consists of three main steps: (a) gathering *domains* (i.e., main topics used to group the data); (b) creating *core ideas* (i.e., summaries of the data that simplify the main points); and (c) *cross-analysis*, a method used to create common themes across all of the study participants (Hill et al., 2005). All members of the team work together in this process of analysis. However, to improve efficiency, when a few cases have been established, individuals can break off in pairs or work independently. The overall goal of CQR data analysis is to distill the meaning of the study participants' words in a cohesive manner. Great care is built into the analysis to check for this cohesiveness. At least one *auditor* (i.e., someone who is not a member of the primary research team) checks all of the material to ensure it falls in the correct domain. In this example, the director of the career center might be a valuable auditor, as she is concerned with the outcome, but offers a different, more removed perspective. Additionally, one of the final steps is the *stability check*, in which two cases that were held from initial cross-analysis are used to determine whether all of the data fits into the created categories. Other final steps include a visual chart of the results and an accuracy check, in which some of the interview transcriptions are sent back to the participants to ensure reliable recording. Reporting the results is similar to other traditional results section where the main purpose is to convey a clear and concise summary. In presenting their findings, researchers may elaborate on one or two case studies to provide a richer contextual perspective (Hill et al., 2005).

Narrative Research

Narrative research is the process of listening to a student's story, and together with the student, creating meaning with respect to the social and cultural context of the story. For career counseling practitioners, this process builds on the intrinsic desires to understand the client's perspective and to help create a better or more functional life situation for them. A story is a series of narrated events. The role of the investigator is to listen to these events and to organize them into a chronological story line with a beginning, middle, and an end. The data can be written up and presented in a story format. This process is valued over the outcome as it engages both the investigator and the participant in working together to determine the meaning of the story. It can be an empowering experience for individuals providing an opportunity for them to voice their own stories (Clandinin & Connelly, 2000). Qualitative inquiry, in general, can be empowering because it involves the participant in an active role as well as honoring and validating a personal story, which may be misunderstood or overlooked by the dominant or mainstream understanding of life and work. Consequently, one main purpose of narrative inquiry is to gain a thorough and deeper understanding of a phenomenon or lived experience (Creswell, 2007).

This experience can be especially powerful for career practitioners working with students whose backgrounds may not fit or represent more traditional modalities. For example, a first-generation student may structure her college experience differently than a traditional student would, perhaps placing more emphasis on finding a certain career or valuing a career opportunity over her current education. By establishing the trust of the student to actively listen to her story in a collaborative manner, the practitioner can gain a deeper understanding of what her experience is beyond that of a general survey. Specifically, listening to another's life events narrows the distance between the two worlds of the practitioner and the student allowing the practitioner to relate to the experience of the student and perhaps find similarities in the human experience. This piece is essential to qualitative inquiry because it acknowledges the differences in worldview and reality that are often taken for granted in more objective measures of evaluation (Hummel, 1991). This new information can then impact existing ways of conceptualizing services and means of evaluation.

The purpose of narrative research is to tell the detailed story of one or a few individuals. A key part is to understand and gather information on the context of the stories to create a comprehensive narrative for the reader. The main process in narrative analysis is *restorying,* or to reorganize the stories into a general framework (Creswell, 2007). Restorying can take different forms, such as determining key elements and placing them in chronological order or in a sequence of implied causality (Carter, 1993). Another aspect of restorying can be to deconstruct the stories, such as pointing out important dichotomies or analyzing contradictions present in the data (Czarniawska, 2004). As mentioned above, narrative analysis is a dual process between the narrator and the researcher where the investigator can confirm meaning with the participant to verify analysis, and both parties can negotiate meaning together (Creswell).

Case Study

Case studies are used widely throughout many fields because their thorough descriptions of a system provide ample data for understanding and explaining phenomena. In educational settings, case studies are commonly used to evaluate the efficiency and effectiveness of initiatives, such as high-risk youth programs and community-based prevention programs (Telis, 1997). In a case study, the data collection process is varied; in depth; and relies on multiple sources of data, such as observations, interviews, documents, and other various artifacts. Although similar to the in-depth nature of a narrative study, a case study specifically examines a bounded system (e.g., an event, process, activity, setting, program, or multiple individuals) with multiple means of information gathering whereas a narrative is limited to a single method of gathering information from an individual. The outcome consists of a report describing the case or multiple cases in full, including central themes that emerge (Creswell, 2007). An *instrumental case study* begins with then selects one context to help illustrate this issue. Similarly, a *collective case study* certain issue as the focus but uses more than one case/context to exemplify it. show several perspectives on the same issue. Lastly, an *intrinsic case study* specific focus, but rather the focus is the case itself (Creswell; Stake, 1994). of investigation is to write a detailed description of each case, often and the chronology of events. Next is the *analysis of themes*, themes that will enhance the understanding of the complexes are being used, then a *cross-case analysis* is used to *case analysis*. The researcher can then create *assertions*, (Creswell, 2007).

might select a case study model to examine the effects of a multiple case study design, practitioners could track the for further robustness of the study and cross-case analysis. selected students determined to be representative of the affected collection process would begin by drawing on many different information interviews with each student held at various times throughout the of documents and archival records could provide a full history and changes.

Considerations in Qualitative Research Design

Understanding the basic overview of the role and purpose of each qualitative model is critical in designing a study to either assess a population or to approach a new perspective or question. This next section addresses common considerations when setting up a research project, such as sampling, how to gain access to a certain population, and the role of the researcher. Lastly, it will describe the many different methods of gathering data from observations, interviews, electronic sources, and other artifacts.

Design Conceptualization

The first step in using qualitative methods is to articulate the reason and value of using more in-depth and descriptive measures over more standardized quantitative measures. Practitioners commonly justify using qualitative methods in their evaluations to seek underlying knowledge and subjective understanding of the issues with which students grapple. For example, it may be helpful to know students' thought processes and reactions to a self-report standardized test measuring their study skills and motivation levels. Although this test draws on direct information from the students, what is unknown is how the students will react to seeing their skill levels compared with a larger population. Another possible justification to use qualitative methods is to highlight the limitations of quantitative methods, such as the fact that research techniques themselves can affect findings (Marshall & Rossman, 2006). For example, a questionnaire format may limit the scope of information elicited from students by suggesting adherence to a predetermined coding of social variables. Also, students filling out a questionnaire may be more likely to adhere to the worldview of the administrator, answering the questions based on what may be expected of them rather than a truthful or more informative answer. Questionnaires can be highly effective measures; however, careful consideration of the effect and desired outcomes should drive the research design. Qualitative methods may also enable an understanding of human behavior that recognizes, rather than limits or ignores, the influence of setting. Practitioners may also choose to use a qualitative method for its exploratory benefits in defining common themes and variable or questions that need to be addressed (Marshall & Rossman).

Sampling

After determining the size of the study to meet the intended purposes, there are many different ways in which an investigator can choose a sample. During *intensity sampling,* an investigator selects participants who wholly represent the issue or phenomenon being studied to elicit rich and in-depth results. Participants drawn from *extreme sampling* represent the farthest end of the spectrum of an issue, also referred to as a unique case. Using an extreme case sampling is justified if it can teach society something useful about the human experience. For example, if a student with a severe mental disorder entered a school system, it might be useful to understand how this experience might shape every day practice, such as how biases professionals might hold toward students labeled with a mental disorder influence their interactions with the student or their choices in the classroom. In *critical case sampling,* the researcher chooses a case that clearly represents the phenomenon and will make a direct point. If the investigator's goal is to capture a variety of perspectives, then *maximum variation sampling* can be used. Additionally, *stratified purposeful sampling* targets all aspects of the population, including below, average, and above average cases. If the researcher has a set of predetermined conditions that will fulfill the task of the study, then *criterion sampling* is appropriate. With *chain sampling* (i.e., snowball technique), the researcher asks for recommendations of people who might fit the study well. *Random sampling* can be used to enhance the credibility of the study, as can *opportunistic sampling*, in which the researcher intentionally chooses new cases during data collection and analysis as a way to take advantage of new possibilities as they arise (Morrow & Smith, 2000; Patton, 1990). To assist the career practitioner in selecting a sampling method, it can be helpful to outline the goals of the study and all possible persons available for sampling and then draw connections indicating which individuals will meet which goals. For example, if the career office wants to gather information on students representing each ethnic group and each gender, then stratified purposeful sampling or criterion sampling would enable the practitioner to meet the needs of the study. If the goal is to evaluate the effect of a class on career development, then intensity sampling would select those students involved in the class. It is important to note that flexibility in sampling is encouraged, as the practitioner may gain new insights in the process of evaluation that can benefit the overall goal of information gathering and meaning making for all participants.

Data Collection in Social Context

Because the investigator takes a more active role in the data collection and analysis in a qualitative study, it is necessary to select the right social context and to gain awareness of how to position oneself to allow for the best process and outcomes. An initial question, which largely depends on the goals of the evaluation process, is to determine how involved the evaluators will be. That choice can range from full participation to passive observation (Marshall & Rossman, 2006). For example, a career counselor interviewing a student in a narrative study context in which the goal is to narrow the gap between the two spheres of understanding may engage in active participation to gain the student's trust. By contrast, an administrative assistant monitoring the length of time and how students use a computer workstation would be involved in more passive observation.

In all situations it is important to be fully aware that the role of the information gatherer is considered an instrument that will have an effect on the evaluation process. Therefore, it is vital for the practitioner to consider his or her impact on the participants while gathering information. Helpful topics for personal and group consideration prior to the evaluation process are reflection of identity and impact on others (e.g., ethnicity, socioeconomic status, religious views); sense of voice (e.g., loud, demanding, passive); assumptions about students (e.g., belief that students of a specific background act in a certain way or follow stereotypes); and personal sensitivities (e.g., past experiences that influence belief systems). All of these considerations are apparent in interactions with others and will affect the data collection process. Other practical questions to consider are (a) what expectation do I have about the evaluation setting, (b) does or how does my role as evaluator differ from my previous role, (c) what is my current comfort level with interacting with others, and (d) what is my ability to fit in to a given role for the purposes of the evaluation process. Asking oneself these questions may seem daunting, however, it will create a closer and a more genuine connection to the perspectives of the population being studied.

Methods of Collecting Data

Observation is one of the oldest methods of data collection, from the roots of qualitative research in anthropology and sociology. Specifically, it is defined as systematic note taking and recording of events, documents, and behaviors in a social setting. Observation methods vary from using structured checklists for tracking recurring behavior patterns and relationships to holistic descriptions of a setting (Marshall & Rossman, 2006). Observing and taking notes and descriptions of the context can lend meaning to an interview and complex interactions in social settings, such as a career counseling center, a classroom, or a retreat.

Interviews range from a standardized set of questions to more flexible and open-ended structures. A practitioner can choose an interview as the only method or in combination with other methods depending on the focus and purpose of the study. An informal interview consists of open-ended questions and is flexible to what the interviewee would like to tell. This method is better at capturing the genuine meaning and words of the participant (i.e., gaining a student's perspective on a topic). Commonly, the practitioner will explore a few general topics but will respect how the interviewee conceptualizes and structures his or her own response (Marshall & Rossman, 2006). Another form of interviewing is focus groups in which the interviewer asks questions to a gathering of individuals. An advantage to using focus groups is the ability to collect rich meaning from the interactions of the participants as they discuss a certain issue (Morrow & Smith, 2000).

Electronic data, such as e-mails, online questionnaires, and discussion groups, are increasingly common and have much information to add to a qualitative study. Although there are pros and cons to this newer form of communication, electronic formats provide the following benefits:

participants may be more likely to share intimate information since responses tend to be anonymous (e.g., in-depth online survey); e-mail and electronic resources may be more convenient (e.g., can be completed at any time of the day, scheduling is less important); and lastly, it may be more efficient as the investigator does not have to transcribe notes (Morrow & Smith, 2000). Disadvantages of using electronic data include the reliance on self-report and honesty, especially when learning about characteristics of those being evaluated, and possible lower response rates due to the lack of face-to-face interaction. Murray and Sixsmith (1998) provide a more extensive discussion of the advantages and disadvantages of electronic data.

Documents and artifacts refer to any relevant physical data, such as art, records, letters, objects, or media recordings (e.g., tapes, videos). This type of data can be used as a primary or secondary source. In career development settings, relevant documents and artifacts may be the students' grades or assignments that can lend alternative perspectives to their career development. In working with an individual in a narrative analysis project, examining artwork or informal drawings of the student can be a rich way to understand the unique context of the individual's life.

Targets for Qualitative Career Assessment and Outcomes

Qualitative career assessment offers many new opportunities to achieve a greater understanding of how individuals think about and move through the world of work. Most notably, qualitative assessment provides a more collaborative working space for the counselor and the client. The power differential between the two is leveled offering the client a chance to become more active and engaged in the process, as well as for the counselor to be a more curious listener rather than an expert and interpreter of meaning (McMahon et al., 2003). This process is especially relevant for career counselors, educators, and administrators as the goal is to seek a closer understanding of clients.

Blustein, Kenna, et al. (2005) offer a review of current qualitative career assessment. Possible targets for career assessment include studying populations that have been excluded or absent from traditional career development or practice; studying general student processes in career development, including subjective meaning of their experiences with the institution as well as their own perceptions of the world of work; and studying staff processes in a career development setting. Qualitative assessment of understudied populations serves to empower and engage such populations as well as to provide rich information and data leading to new assessments. Current qualitative career assessment focusing on understudied populations include women of color (Gomez et al., 2001; Richie et al., 1997); persons with disabilities (Noonan et al., 2004); noncollege bound youth (Blustein, Phillips, et al., 1997); and the impact of family, friends, and spouses on career-related topics (Schultheiss, 2005). In college and university settings, there are many targets for qualitative research, including first-generation college students, students of color, international students, students within a specific major, and nontraditional students.

Conclusion

Learning more about qualitative methods of evaluation and beginning to use them in program research and assessment will enhance the meaning and depth of information gathering in a career development setting. Often qualitative methods mimic practitioners' own sense of curiosity and involvement in students' lives and can serve as a rewarding way to conduct useful evaluations. Qualitative methods focus on the use of relationship in learning, a value upheld with those employed in student services. Bringing awareness to the role of relationships in research creates a more natural setting for both practitioner and student to interact and ultimately to gain information and promote growth. Lastly, central to working with an array of students, using qualitative methods will assist the practitioner in better understanding the dynamics of students' lives, enhancing the understanding of integral processes (e.g., how students chose a major or what barriers exist for entering a career counseling center). Used alone or in combination with quantitative techniques, qualitative methodology can provide greater meaning and depth of information gathering in a career development study or enhance more traditional methods of evaluation of key process within an institution.

References

Blustein, D. L., Kenna, A. C., Murphy, M. A., DeVoy, J. E., & DeWine, D. B. (2005). Qualitative research in career development: Exploring the center and margins of discourse about careers and working. *Journal of Career Assessment, 13,* 351-370.

Blustein, D. L., Phillips, S. D., Jobin-Davis, K., Finkelberg, S. L., & Roarke, A. E. (1997). A theory-building investigation of the school-to-work transition. *The Counseling Psychologist, 25,* 364-402.

Carter, K. (1993). The place of a story in the study of teaching and teacher education. *Educational Researcher, 22,* 5-12.

Clandinin, D. J., & Connelly, F. M. (2000). *Narrative inquiry: Experience and story in qualitative research.* San Francisco, CA: Jossey-Bass.

Creswell, J. W. (2007). *Qualitative inquiry and research design: Choosing among five approaches* (2nd ed.). Thousand Oaks, CA: Sage.

Czarniawska, B. (2004). *Narrative in social science research.* London, UK: Sage.

Glaser, B., & Strauss, A. (1967). *The discovery of grounded theory: Strategies for qualitative research.* Chicago, IL: Aldine De Gruyther.

Gomez, M. J., Fassinger, R.E., Prosser, J., Cooke, K., Meija, B., & Luna, J. (2001). Voces abriendo caminos (voices forging paths): A qualitative study of the career development of notable Latinas. *Journal of Counseling Psychology, 48,* 286-300.

Hill, C. E., Knox, S., Thompson, B. J., Hess, S. A., Ladany, N., Williams, E. N. (2005). Consensual qualitative research: An update. *Journal of Counseling Psychology, 52,* 196-205.

Hill, C., Thompson, B., & Williams, E. (1997). A guide to conducting consensual qualitative research. *The Counseling Psychologist, 25,* 517-572.

Hummel, R. P. (1991). Stories managers tell: Why they are valid as science. *Public Administration Review, 51,* 31-41.

Marshall, C., & Rossman, G. B. (2006). *Designing qualitative research* (4th ed.). Thousand Oaks, CA: Sage.

McMahon, M., Patton, W., & Watson, M. (2003). Developing qualitative career assessment processes. *The Career Development Quarterly, 51,* 194-202.

Morrow, S. L., & Smith, M. L. (2000). Qualitative research for counseling psychology. In S. D. Brown & R. W. Lent (Eds.), *Handbook of counseling psychology* (3rd ed., pp. 199-230). New York, NY: John Wiley.

Murray, C. D., & Sixsmith, J. (1998). E-mail: A qualitative research medium for interviewing? *International Journal of Social Research Methodology Theory and Practice, 1,* 103-121.

Noonan, B. M., Gallor, S. M., Hensler-McGinns, N. F., Fassinger, R. E., Wang, S., & Goodman, J. (2004). Challenge and success: A qualitative study of the career development of highly achieving women with physical and sensory disabilities. *Journal of Counseling Psychology, 51,* 68-80.

Patton, M. Q. (1990). *Qualitative education and research methods* (2nd ed.). Newbury Park, CA: Sage.

Richie, B. S., Fassinger, R. E., Linn, S. G., Johnson, J., Prosser, J., & Robinson, S. (1997). Persistence, connection and passion: A qualitative study of the career development of highly achieving African American/Black and White women. *Journal of Counseling Psychology, 44*, 133-148.

Schultheiss, D. E. P. (2005). Qualitative relational career assessment: A constructivist paradigm. *Journal of Career Assessment, 13*, 381-394.

Stake, R. E. (1994). Case studies. In N. K. Denzin & Y. S. Lincoln (Eds.) *Handbook of qualitative research* (pp. 175-188). Thousand Oaks, CA: Sage.

Strauss, A. & Corbin, J. (1990). *Basics of qualitative research: Grounded theory, procedures, and techniques.* Newbury Park, CA: Sage.

Strauss, A., & Corbin, J. (1998). *Basics of qualitative research* (2nd ed.). Newbury Park, CA: Sage.

Subich, L. M. (1996). Addressing diversity in the process of career assessment. In M. L. Savickas & W. B. Walsh (Eds.), *Handbook of career counseling theory and practice* (pp. 277-289). Palo Alto, CA: Davies-Black.

Tellis, W. (1997, July). Introduction to case study. *The Qualitative Report* [On-line serial], *3*(2). Retrieved from http://www.nova.edu/ssss/QR/QR3-2/tellis1.html

Additional Resources

Qualitative Career Assessment

McMahon, M., Watson, M., & Patton, W. (2005). Qualitative career assessment: Developing the My System of Career Influences Reflection Activity. *Journal of Career Assessment, 13*, 476-490.

Whiston, S., & Rahardja, D. (2005). Qualitative career assessment: An overview and analysis. *Journal of Career Assessment, 13*, 371-380.

Qualitative Research Methods and Study Design

Bogdan, R. C., & Biklen, S. K. (2003). *Qualitative research for education: An introduction to theory and methods* (4th ed.) Boston, MA: Allyn & Bacon.

Fontana, A., & Frey, J. H. (1994). Interviewing. In N. K. Denzin & Y. S. Lincoln (Eds.) *Handbook of qualitative research* (pp. 361-376). Thousand Oaks, CA: Sage.

Qualitative Research and Action Research

Hollingsworth, S. (Ed.). (1997). *International action research: A casebook for educational reform.* London, UK: Falmer.

Stringer, E. T. (1999). *Action research: A handbook for practitioners* (2nd ed.). Thousand Oaks, CA: Sage.

CHAPTER 5

CAREER DEVELOPMENT OUTCOMES: VARIABLES AND INSTRUMENTS ACROSS THE COLLEGE EXPERIENCE

Wade C. Leuwerke and Bengü Ergüner-Tekinalp

Career development is a central aspect, and arguably the primary goal, of the college experience. Comprehensive career planning efforts span the entire college experience. Measurement of these processes can begin before the student steps foot on campus and continue for years after graduation. Effective measurement of career outcomes demonstrates how coursework, advising, and career development interventions impact students. As such, it should be an essential focus of faculty and student services personnel. This chapter briefly defines and reviews assessment, explains common career development constructs, and explores mechanisms that postsecondary institutions might create to examine those constructs. Descriptions of available instruments and common practices for assessing career development are also offered. The chapter concludes with a discussion of approaches for evaluating a career development program.

Career Assessment Process

The purpose of career assessment is to gather career-related information from individuals and help them clarify interests, values, self-efficacy beliefs, and goals; develop career plans; and engage in the career decision-making process. Assessment, in general, provides information to professionals (e.g., advisors, professors, counselors) to create learning opportunities and targeted career development interventions that address students' developmental needs. It is a learning process for both the professionals and the students (Sampson, Reardon, Peterson, & Lenz, 2004).

Different terms are used to describe assessment processes and procedures. Evaluation, assessment, testing, measurement, and outcome are related concepts and often used interchangeably. Biggs (1994) defined assessment as "a set of procedures used for developing impressions, images, making decisions, and checking hypotheses about the pattern of characteristics that determines a person's behavior in interactions with the environment" (p. 26). Other chapters in this volume will note that assessment includes evaluation of the effectiveness or efficacy of a practice. For this chapter, career assessment encompasses the definition above.

Measurement, testing, evaluation, and outcomes are all aspects of the assessment process. The term measurement describes either categorizing events (qualitative) or assigning numerical values to traits, attributes, or characteristics (quantitative). Generally, a standard scale is applied to provide a numerical score with quantitative data (Fawcett, 2007). Testing involves the use of specific instruments or procedures to gather information (Neukrug & Fawcett, 2009). Evaluation incorporates clinical or professional judgment about the individual into the assessment process (Fawcett). Outcome refers to the end result of an intervention; well-defined outcomes are specific, observable, and measurable. They are ideally defined before the intervention and measured using a test or process that determines the effect or change in the targeted characteristic or attribute. Combining these features, assessment can be described as a process that involves multiple methods of information gathering, including testing, evaluation, and measurement of outcomes to help the professional (a) understand the individual, (b) draw conclusions about interventions, and (c) evaluate the effectiveness of those efforts.

Central Tenets of Assessment

Creating an effective assessment plan requires understanding the basic concepts that underlie the measurement and testing process. Central among these are reliability and validity, standardized or nonstandardized procedures, the use of qualitative or quantitative data, and norm-referenced and scale-score comparison procedures. Reliability refers to how consistently the measurement procedures produce similar results. For instance, a scale may consistently measure a bunch of bananas at two pounds. To the extent the scale consistently produces this result it would be regarded as reliable. Validity is concerned with the accuracy of the measurement or the extent to which the procedure is measuring what it claims to measure. If the procedures yield the height of the bananas when aiming to assess weight, then the scale would not be valid, as it is not measuring what it claims to measure. In terms of human functioning, validity is concerned with accurately measuring the construct under consideration. If an interest inventory actually measures individuals' vocational interests, then it would be considered valid. If that instrument were tapping into individuals' exposure to different occupations, rather than vocational interest, it would not be measuring what it claimed to measure. As such, it would not be valid. A measure, inventory, or scale can maintain its reliability while not being valid, but an unreliable measure can never have validity.

Standardized tests are tools that are designed for a specific purpose with a set of unchanging procedures that include instructions on how to administer, score, and interpret the results (Cole, Finch, Gowland, & Mayo, 1995). Standardized tests aim for minimal variation in administration, which supports the reliability and validity of the instrument or procedure. Many of the instruments described in this chapter are standardized tests. Nonstandardized tests are those that do not have specific requirements on how the material is administered to test takers. Also, the scoring and interpretive procedures do not follow specific, predetermined protocols. For example, a card sort procedure involves arranging a set of cards with different stimuli based on specific criteria. A work values card sort has individuals categorize work values (e.g., prestige, flexibility, salary) based on the importance of attaining each variable in an occupation. Through sorting and discussion, the individual identifies the personal significance of each value without comparison to how others might respond to the same criteria. Standardization is critical for the mass distribution of a test as it allows for comparison of different individuals in different settings to a normative sample. Nonstandardized approaches are ideal in situations where purchase of a standardized test is unrealistic or the audience for the assessment results is local stakeholders concerned with assessing program or intervention effectiveness (e.g., institutional administrators).

Assessment can involve the gathering of qualitative or quantitative data. Qualitative data includes information that is collected and expressed in nonnumerical ways (Goldman, 1990). This type of data is often descriptive and frequently more detailed and information rich. An example would be to ask students to write a paragraph describing their ideal job. The data produced from this process might include job titles, work environments, daily activities, and work values. Quantitative data capture numerical expression of phenomena that are being measured. Traits, attributes, and beliefs are represented by numbers or scores on a scale. A quantitative measure of job searching self-efficacy might ask respondents to rate their confidence in creating a résumé, writing a cover letter, and successfully completing an interview. Larger numerical scores on such a scale would represent higher self-efficacy to complete tasks necessary to find a job. Quantitative data provide specific and comparable information in the measurement process.

Deriving meaning from test scores requires a process for drawing conclusions about what is meant by either the quantitative or qualitative data that resulted from completing a career measure. Norm-referenced tests compare an individual's scores to a large sample of people who have completed the same instrument. Scores on norm-referenced measures foster understanding of how much or what type of trait the individual possesses. For example, a norm-referenced measure of career indecision compares the test taker to a large population of people ranging from completely decided to highly undecided. Many commercially available instruments, such as the Strong Interest Inventory (SII; Donnay, Morris, Schaubhut, & Thompson, 2005), are norm-referenced measures.

Understanding the meaning of a measure can also be done by examining scale scores from nonnormed instruments. As with the job searching self-efficacy example above, higher scale scores might suggest that an individual possesses more of the trait being measured. These types of instruments are less generalizable than norm-referenced tests but do provide valuable information to students, faculty, and student services personnel. Drawing conclusions from qualitative measurement is often done at the individual or small-group level. An instructor who assigns students to write a paper about job searching self-efficacy might evaluate the data for responses that indicate increased confidence in completing specific tasks (e.g., I am able to create a professional résumé). Through these mechanisms, assessment fosters greater understanding of individuals and supports data-driven career decision making.

Career Variables and Measures

This section defines commonly assessed career constructs and identifies the instruments frequently used to measure each variable. Information is also provided on low-cost and possibly free mechanisms to measure each construct as well as examples of how and when each may be assessed in a college student population. The discussion concludes with a review of factors to consider when selecting an instrument.

Vocational Interests

Vocational or career interests represent an individual's liking or inclination to perform the job duties required for a specific occupation (e.g., help others, repair equipment, investigate problems) and the appeal of the content of the career (e.g., science, math, business, human development). Super (1957) suggested interests can be manifested as verbal statements (e.g., I enjoy architecture.); expressed through actions (e.g., enrolling in an industrial arts course); or estimated through the use of interest inventories. Holland's (1997) theory of person-environment fit is arguably the predominant model of career interests. His taxonomy organizes individuals into combinations of six personality or interest types, commonly known as RIASEC (i.e., realistic, investigative, artistic, social, enterprising, and conventional). Work environments can be categorized into the same six types. Person-environment fit is based on the concept that as an individual gathers more information about both their own interests as well as the requirements of different work environments, they are more likely to be drawn to occupations that match or are congruent with their interests. The person-environment fit theory suggests that individuals with more defined interest patterns, who select occupations or academic majors that are congruent with those interests, are more likely to be satisfied in their choice and are more likely to persist.

There are a large number of interest inventories available, ranging in length, complexity, administration mechanism, and price. The SII (Donnay et al., 2005) and the Self-Directed Search (SDS; Holland, Fritzsche, & Powell, 1994) are two popular tools that measure interests using the RIASEC model. The SII is administered through paper and pencil, by computer, or online. The instrument is computer scored, and a lengthy, multiscale report is generated, which can be interpreted individually or in group or classroom formats. The SII provides a comprehensive assessment of interests, and the interpretive report presents results on a student's or client's general and specific interests as well as similarity to individuals employed in a wide range of occupations. The SDS is a shorter and more affordable self-administered instrument that produces a three-letter code using the RIASEC system. The SDS is an optimal choice when resources are limited, a large number of individuals need assessment, and a basic identification of interests is required. This instrument can be used in conjunction with *The Occupations Finder* (Holland, 1996) to help students identify careers that are consistent with their interests. The SDS is one of the most economical and easily administered interest inventories available. Students, instructors, or advisors can readily score and then discuss the results through individual or group formats. An alternative, low-cost mechanism to assist students in identifying career interests would encompass providing a broad list of occupations organized by the six RIASEC types. Such lists can be found online or by talking with an experienced career counselor. Students could rate their level of interest in each occupation included in the lists and, using the raw scores, create a three-letter interest profile based on the strength of the rating for the six types.

The Unisex Edition of the ACT Interest Inventory (UNIACT; ACT, Inc., 2009) is another widely administered interest inventory. This instrument is often administered with the ACT test, resulting in a large number of students completing the inventory. The UNIACT organizes interests into six basic scales analogous to Holland's hexagon. Interests are further organized into 26 occupational clusters displayed on the World of Work Map (ACT, Inc., 2009). Institutions that require students to provide an ACT score as part of the application process may be able to access students' UNIACT assessment results and use this information in the career development process.

There are a variety of other interest inventories available, both traditional paper and pencil formats as well as online assessments. Many universities have access to career development products that include interest inventories along with skills and values assessments. Some of the most common are Discover, the Kuder Career Planning System (KCPS), and Choices. There are also many stand-alone interest inventories, including the Campbell Interests and Skills Survey, O*NET Interest Profiler, Career Decision-Making System, and the Career Occupational Preference System.

Completion and interpretation of an interest assessment can be done several times during students' college experience. Many first-year seminars include a comprehensive career development unit, which often begins with an interest assessment. Students, first- to junior-year, who are seeking assistance with selecting a major, are prime candidates for completing an interest assessment. Seniors may also benefit from completion of an interest assessment to target specific occupations within the broad field that may encompass their major area of study. An interest assessment could be used in a pre-posttest format to evaluate the effectiveness of a career intervention designed to help undecided students explore and then narrow their career interests. Factors to consider when choosing an instrument include the time and money available to administer and purchase an instrument, as well as personal preferences for organizing interests according to Holland's (1997) hexagon or career clusters.

Values

In the vocational realm, values constitute goals or desired end states that individuals would like to experience in their occupation, as well as how the person will achieve the desired outcomes. Work values encompass many of the environmental rewards and punishments that people experience in their jobs. For instance, someone who highly values a fast-paced, varied, and social environment may feel quite rewarded in a sales position that includes new challenges each day. Conversely, the same individual is likely to be distressed in an office setting that requires him or her to spend eight hours interacting with a computer, performing repetitious and monotonous tasks. Social Cognitive Career Theory (SCCT; Lent, Brown, & Hackett, 1994) incorporates values into outcome expectations, which are the anticipated consequences for performing a specific behavior. Integrated into the major and career choice process, an individual who values financial prosperity and respect may select a major in business management or premed that will prepare him or her for a career as a chief financial officer or a radiologist, both high-paying, well-regarded occupations.

There are a small number of standard tests that assess values and are available to purchase as part of a career development intervention. The Minnesota Importance Questionnaire (MIQ; Gay, Weiss, Hendel, Dawis, & Lofquist, 1971) assesses six values (i.e., achievement, altruism, autonomy, comfort, safety, and status), which are further divided into 20 needs (e.g., social status, creativity, independence). The MIQ report compares the student's values and needs with reinforcers identified in 185 different occupations, providing a measure of similarity between the individual and occupations. The Values Scale (VS; Nevill & Super, 1989) is a 105-item instrument that assesses the importance of 21 different work values, including economic reward, physical activity, risk, and variety. The VS is a paper and pencil instrument that can be hand scored and interpreted in individual or group formats. The choice of a values assessment will be impacted by access to training in how to use the instrument, the level of detail desired through the assessment process, and time to score the instrument. The MIQ assesses both work values and needs but requires computer scoring. Conversely, the VS measures 21 values but can be scored by hand.

Work values assessment can be accomplished using informal methods through the creation of a list of work values and descriptions, (e.g., independence—the ability to work on your own and set your own goals with minimal or no supervision). Students would be instructed to rate the importance of each value in their future career. The highest rated items can be discussed with students or serve as the basis for a research activity that would require examining potential careers to determine the extent to which the value is reinforced in each occupation. Information in the *Occupational Outlook Handbook* (*OOH*; U.S. Department of Labor, 2010-2011) can serve as a resource to examine and compare careers to identified values.

Another low cost method for examining work values is a card sort activity. Values and descriptions are printed on index cards. Students, individually or in groups, are then guided through an activity to organize or sort the cards based on the importance of each value. One approach requires students to identify their top 10 values. Students are then led through a guided imagery exercise that begins with them being hired in their ideal career that provides or reinforces all 10 values. Through a sequence of steps, the imagined position deteriorates (e.g., economic down turn, poor leadership, increased competition), and one at a time, students relinquish their values to keep their job. At the end, the students will have a ranked list of their top 10 values based on the order they were discarded. In a group setting, many students can participate in the activity and then share their experience with the group. Individually, each student is able to explore and focus on his or her own reaction to the exercise and share this experience with the career development professional.

Work values assessment is an ideal complement to formal interest assessment and can be completed as part of a comprehensive career development intervention at any time during a student's college career. Values assessment may be particularly useful as students complete their college education and are considering specific career paths. Examination of which values will or will not be supported in different occupations is crucial information to those entering the work force. Students who are considering dropping out of college may also benefit from careful review of their work values. Discovering the benefits of a college degree in securing a desirable work environment is valuable information for confused or unmotivated students.

Self-Efficacy Beliefs

During the past few decades, self-efficacy has become a significant factor in career development theories, assessment, and interventions. Self-efficacy refers to an individual's confidence in their ability to perform tasks required to achieve a desired performance goal (Bandura, 1986). Self-efficacy beliefs can be measured for any college-related tasks. For instance, an individual holds a certain level of confidence in her ability to successfully perform a classroom presentation. Another student may hold low confidence, or self-efficacy, in his ability to earn a *B* or higher in his sociology class. Self-efficacy impacts performance through motivation, persistence, and tactics to perform the task. A student with higher confidence is more likely to be initially motivated and maintain that drive during the task. Further, individuals with high self-efficacy have likely had successful experiences performing the task in the past and are able to draw upon these events to understand how to accomplish a similar task in the future.

Self-efficacy beliefs should be defined and measured at a narrow level of specificity. It is appropriate to measure self-efficacy for specific tasks, (e.g., deliver a presentation) while it is not meaningful to assess more global goals (e.g., have a happy life). The combination of self-efficacy and interests has been found to be a valid predictor of individuals' choice of academic majors and careers (Betz et al., 2003). Self-efficacy accounts for the student's view of his or her ability to perform tasks associated with majors and careers. Therefore, incorporation of self-efficacy is valuable, as it provides an additional dimension to the career decision-making process.

One avenue of self-efficacy assessment that has emerged is the measurement of beliefs that correspond to career interest types. The Kuder Skills Assessment (KSA; Zytowski & Luzzo, 2002) measures confidence on six scales that coincide with the six interest clusters in the KCPS. The Expanded Skills Confidence Inventory (ECSI; Betz et al., 2003) measures self-efficacy for career-related activities with a greater degree of specificity, providing results on 17 scales more consistent with the Basic Interest Scales on the SII. These instruments are accessible as part of larger career development systems and may serve as useful measures at institutions with existing access to the programs.

Other approaches to self-efficacy assessment have focused on specific aspects of the college experience. Recently developed measures of noncognitive factors that impact student success and retention have incorporated a scale that measures an individual's confidence to successfully complete academic activities in college (e.g., earn a *B* average during the first semester of college). The Student Readiness Inventory (SRI; ACT, Inc., 2008) includes the Academic Self-Confidence Scale, and the Student Strengths Inventory (SSI; Gore, Brown, Leuwerke, & Metz, 2008) has an Academic Self-Efficacy scale. Self-efficacy in math, science, technology, and engineering has been widely studied, and consequently, a number of assessments have been developed for these areas (Betz & Hackett, 1983; Lent, Brown, & Larkin, 1984). Finally, the Career Decision Self-Efficacy Scale (CDSE; Betz, Hammond, & Multon, 2005) measures confidence for engaging in tasks associated with making a career choice, such as self-appraisal, occupational information, goal setting, planning, and problem solving.

Self-efficacy is a construct that can be measured using informal methods. The critical factor in developing such techniques is to assess specific behavioral domains. Gore and Leuwerke (2000) assessed self-efficacy for tasks associated with career interests, creating lists of occupations organized by the six RIASEC types and asking students to rate how confident (i.e., not confident to highly confident) they were in their ability to successfully complete the requirements to obtain each career. Similar assessments could be designed by instructors or career and student services personnel, asking students to rate their ability to successfully complete a first-year seminar, choose an academic major, learn new study skills, obtain an internship, effectively use student services available on campus, complete a capstone course, or prepare a résumé.

Students' self-efficacy for performing academic- and career-related behaviors can be assessed across the college experience in a multitude of different behavior domains. For example, academic self-efficacy could be assessed during first-year orientation, and students with low scores could then be directed to the tutoring center. Other relevant interventions designed to strengthen self-efficacy can also be woven into the first-year seminar. Self-efficacy could be measured again at the end of the first semester to determine how well tutoring or the seminar strengthened students' confidence.

Other examples include using a nonstandard measure of self-efficacy coupled with an interest assessment as part of a comprehensive career development outreach program for undecided sophomores or assessing juniors who have completed internships. Using before and after self-efficacy assessments of an internship can provide useful information related to students' confidence in their ability to enter the world of work, communicate with coworkers, effectively manage their time, and successfully complete tasks as expected. Specific internship activities might also be assessed. For example, marketing majors could be assessed on their confidence in planning a marketing campaign, conducting a needs assessment, evaluating market research, effectively communicating with clients/customers, and delivering a final campaign. Alternatively, education majors could rate their ability to create lesson plans, manage a classroom, handle student concerns, and consult with colleagues and parents after their semester as a student teacher.

Career Maturity

Students' readiness to engage in the career-development and decision-making process are impacted by their level of career maturity, which involves the ability or willingness to self-evaluate, gather information on the world of work, and make career decisions. Super (1983) identified five dimensions of career maturity: (a) planfulness—knowledge of how to create a plan, (b) exploration—collecting information about one's self, (c) information gathering—obtaining information about the world of work, (d) decision making—choosing a career based on objective information, and (e) reality orientation—making realistic career decisions and demonstrating consistency of choice.

Levinson, Ohler, Caswell, and Kiewra (1998) reviewed six measures of career maturity. For example, the Career Maturity Inventory-Revised (CMI-R; Crites & Savickas, 1996) includes 25-item attitude and competence subscales. Students agree or disagree with each item; more agreement statements indicate increasing career maturity. The Career Beliefs Inventory (CBI) and the Career Decision Scale (CDS), both reviewed below, can also be used as a measure of career maturity (Levinson et al.). The CBI measures a broad range of thoughts about the career development process and may be a feasible approach if several aspects of career development problems are being evaluated.

Career maturity can also be measured through locally developed approaches. Counselors and instructors can work with students to explore the student's readiness to engage in the career development process, as well as level of knowledge about self and the world of work. Students could rate the extent developmental statements (e.g., I am ready to make a career/major choice today or

I possess adequate information about the world of work to make an informed career/major choice) fit their current situation. This approach would be well suited to a pretest, posttest evaluation model for an intervention or class designed to increase maturity and readiness to make a career choice.

Students encounter difficulties from low career maturity throughout the college experience. During the first year, career maturity assessment can help students identify where to focus their attention and assist them in making informed career choices. First-year students high in career maturity may benefit from interventions that support exploration and solidification of their career choice. Those low in maturity will benefit from developmentally appropriate approaches that help them self-explore as well as learn how to make career choices. As sophomores, these students can then spend the second year of college exploring different majors and occupations to build their knowledge of the world of work. Junior and senior students who have very low career maturity may benefit from more intensive interventions to help them acquire self and world-of-work information as well as skill development in the areas of planning and decision making.

Career Indecision

Career indecision encompasses an individual's difficulty in making a career choice. The construct is most frequently conceptualized to include cognitive and affective components. Cognitive aspects of indecision include lack of information about self and the world of work. Affective limits include anxiety about making a career choice and broad decision-making difficulties. Gati, Krausz, and Osipow (1996) developed a model that identified career indecision problems based on readiness to make a choice; career information deficits (i.e., self, world of work, and decision-making process); and information problems (i.e., incorrect or conflicting career information).

The Career Decision Scale (CDS; Osipow, 1987) is a brief, self-scored measure of indecision that includes a 2-item certainty scale and a 16-item indecision scale. The Career Factors Inventory (CFI; Chartrand, Robbins, Morrill, & Boggs, 1990) is a 21-item measure of indecision that assesses two affective factors (i.e., choice anxiety and general indecisiveness) and two cognitive aspects (i.e., need for career information and need for self knowledge). The Career Decision-Making Difficulties Questionnaire (CDDQ; Osipow & Gati, 1998) is a 44-item assessment of indecision based on Gati et al.'s (1996) taxonomy.

A career-indecision measure could readily be developed at a local level using the components noted above and asking students to rate the extent to which each aspect is prohibiting them from making a career choice. It is also possible that attributes of the campus population might be contributing to career indecision. An institution with a substantial population of first-generation college students may encounter many students with very little information about the world of work or incorrect information about the educational requirements to enter certain occupations. An institution-specific measure could measure these attributes.

Another strategy is to incorporate career indecision into a comprehensive career development program offered at any time during college. Indecision may be intentionally addressed in a career-development class or in a career counseling session. In a broad assessment approach, an indecision measure can help identify students who may need more specific, individual interventions to address factors that are contributing to decision-making difficulties. Once indecisive students are identified, a standardized measure may be appropriate to more specifically determine which aspect(s) may be creating barriers for the individual.

Career Development Problems

There are a number of instruments designed to identify or diagnose problems that individuals experience during the career decision-making or development process. These tools aim to measure cognitive aspects or beliefs about career development that are creating impediments to choice or planning processes. Obviously, the potential problems that individuals might perceive as barriers to career development vary widely. This breadth is reflected in the number of subscales on these measures, including overcoming obstacles, responsibility for career choice (Career Beliefs Inventory), decision-making confusion, commitment anxiety (Career Thoughts Inventory), lack of confidence, and disability/health concerns (Career Barriers Inventory – Revised).

The Career Beliefs Inventory (CBI; Krumboltz, 1991) is a 96-item instrument that identifies thoughts about career that are limiting the individual. There are 25 different subscales, which are organized into five headings that focus on aspects such as career development status and effort required to move forward. The Career Thoughts Inventory (CTI; Sampson, Peterson, Lenz, Reardon, & Saunders, 1996) is a 48-item measure designed to evaluate thoughts that may be hindering career development. The test reports a total score and three subscale scores. The CTI packet comes with a workbook that is designed to assist students in addressing the negative cognitions that are impeding development. The Career Barriers Inventory – Revised (CBI-R; Swanson, Daniels, & Tokar, 1996) is a 70-item instrument that reports barriers on 13 subscales. The CBI-R encompasses subscales that measure aspects that are internal (e.g., inadequate preparation) as well as external to the individual (e.g., sex discrimination, job market constraints).

The problems and negative beliefs that students encounter before, during, or after college may be readily assessed at the local level. Voices across the campus will have outstanding input to facilitate the creation of an institution-specific measure of career development problems. A checklist of obstacles is a possible measurement approach using items offered by students, faculty, and student services personnel of the most common difficulties experienced by students at key transition points. These statements could then be collated and organized into a list for students to use to identify impediments. Further, interventions can be created to address specific concerns. The career services office may be particularly adept at addressing résumé building and interviewing obstacles, and all campus stakeholders would then know to refer students who identify these difficulties to the appropriate office.

Career development concerns will surface across the college experience. A comprehensive, campus-wide effort to address these issues might expand on the locally devised checklist above by administering the instrument to the entire student body each year. The results of the assessment could be distributed to each student with referrals to the campus resources that have designed interventions to address identified concerns. This process might be particularly helpful for senior students if the instrument includes common problems experienced by former students in the years following graduation. Institutions can then develop and provide programs to address the challenges students are likely to encounter after college, such as how to network or negotiate a benefits package successfully.

Instrument Selection

As evidenced above, numerous instruments are available to student services personnel and faculty interested in assessing students' career development. The process of selecting a measurement should consider the reliability, validity, and cross-cultural fairness of the instrument or method. When selecting standardized, commercially available products, research documenting the psychometric properties of the instrument (i.e., its reliability and validity) should be readily accessible. All other factors being equal, measures with stronger reliability and validity are preferable choices. Cross-cultural fairness (i.e., the extent to which the test is free from bias) also needs to be evaluated when reviewing instruments.

In addition, several practical and logistical factors should also be evaluated in making these decisions. These include cost, test format, administration and scoring time, training and expertise to interpret results, and customizability. The setting and personnel involved in the assessment process will guide much of this decision-making process. In a classroom or group setting, paper and pencil assessments that can be easily scored and returned for a subsequent meeting might be ideal. Students in classes with computer access can more easily complete Internet-based assessments. Instructor expertise in career development and test analysis and the availability of other professionals (e.g., career or counseling center staff or counseling graduate students) to provide group interpretation will also influence the selection of tools. Individual career counseling settings may permit greater reliance on the expertise of student services personnel to administer, score, and interpret results to students.

Further, faculty and staff should consider the customizability of both the instrument and student feedback mechanisms. Some standardized career assessment programs (e.g., Kuder Career System) contain different tests that allow administration of only the instruments that match the goals of the career intervention. Idiographic approaches and locally developed instruments support customization to specific individuals, groups, or classes depending on the variables of interest. Finally, instruments such as the SSI allow users to customize the student feedback report to direct students to take different action steps depending on their results.

Career Program Evaluation

There are numerous approaches to examining the effectiveness and outcomes of career development interventions. This section describes three different designs that can be used to measure the impact of systematic career development activities. The importance of identifying outcomes and attending to multicultural aspects in the assessment process is also addressed.

Program Evaluation Design

Pretest, posttest design is intended to measure the effectiveness of a program. Participants are given the tests before the program starts and when the program ends. The results are then compared. The strength of this design is that the changes facilitated by the program can be more directly attributed to the intervention as the individuals' outcome scores are compared, using the same scale, to pre-intervention scores (Kazdin, 2003). Pretest measurement can also be used as a selection tool to determine appropriateness of participation or for placement into specific groups within the intervention (Heppner, Wampold, & Kivlighan, 2008).

Posttest-only design is also used to evaluate the effectiveness of a program. Participants are given the test at the end of the program. Without pretest information, it is more difficult to attribute outcomes to the specific intervention. However, if control or comparison groups are available, this provides another mechanism to test for program effects. If program participants demonstrate posttest outcomes that are substantially different from the control or comparison group, this provides evidence for the effects of the intervention.

Idiographic measurement is a locally developed assessment approach that is tailored and unique to the individual, providing a phenomenological perspective. Asking a student to give a detailed explanation of careers in which he or she is interested, rank aspects of careers based on their appeal, or state a personal goal of going through a career services program are all examples of idiographic stimuli. During the measurement process, students respond to the test items that were created specifically for them, and individuals rate their progress or outcome on these stimuli to measure the effectiveness of an intervention.

An example of idiographic measurement would be a career advisor asking a client to write down specific goals (e.g., I will create a complete, professional résumé) at the beginning of counseling that become the items evaluated to determine the outcome of the intervention. Using a Likert scale, the student rates the extent to which each goal has been achieved at various points during the counseling sessions. The measurement provides specific information to the student on the progress toward his or her individualized objectives, and scores from all clients, on their personally created outcome measures, could also be accumulated to demonstrate the effectiveness of counselors in helping clients achieve their desired career development goals.

Identifying Outcomes

The assessment of career development programs requires particular attention to defining the specific outcomes to be measured and evaluated. Whether it is an idiographic measure or a norm-referenced inventory, effective assessment requires clear articulation of intended results. Attention to critical aspects of outcome definition (i.e., objective, specific, measurable, behavioral, and attainable) will greatly enhance the potential for accurately documenting the effects of a career development intervention. Targets that are more proximal, or closer in time, to the intervention are more easily measured. For example, a career exploration class for sophomore health sciences majors might identify and measure the following career development goals: (a) students will create a career development plan by the end of the semester; (b) students will complete an assessment battery (e.g., CBI, SII, MIQ, Health Careers Self-Efficacy) and receive an interpretation from a career counselor; and (c) students will attend three meetings with their academic advisors to plan appropriate coursework for the following three semesters. Articulating clear, specific objectives prior to a career intervention greatly increases the probability of demonstrating that students achieve the desired outcome.

Multicultural Considerations

In a diverse and rapidly changing world, it is important to attend to students' cultural backgrounds and account for these in the career assessment process. The definition of culture should encompass anything that makes an individual unique. Characteristics to consider include race, ethnicity, disability, religion, gender, sexual orientation, and national origin. D'Andrea and Daniels (2001) suggest being cognizant of multiple aspects that significantly influence individual's development. In their RESPECTFUL counseling model they identified 10 factors that impact a person's psychological development and sense of personal well being. These factors are religious-spiritual identity (R), ethnic-cultural-racial background (E), sexual identity (S), psychological maturity (P), economic class (E), chronological-developmental challenges (C), threats to one's personal well being (T), family history and dynamics (F), unique physical characteristics (U), and location of residence (L). To reduce the potential for misunderstanding and harm from the assessment process related to diversity issues, professionals need to

 ◇ Develop an awareness of norm-referenced samples of standardized tests and their appropriateness to the student being assessed

- Make a conscious effort not to minimize or overemphasize the influence of culture with each student
- Examine the impact of the assessor's culture in the dynamic among all participants
- Use culturally appropriate tests and measurement procedures
- Account for possible cultural differences in the interpretation process
- Consider idiographic and qualitative approaches when norm-referenced samples negate the appropriateness of an instrument
- Evaluate interest assessment domains for applicability to both collectivist and individualistic cultures

Contemplation of the many facets of multicultural assessment will help ensure an equal and accurate process for all students.

Conclusion

There are a wide variety of constructs related to the career development process. Accurate and effective measurement of these variables requires a solid grounding in the assessment process, thorough understanding of variables of interest, and a well-articulated and executed assessment plan. A number of free and low-cost measures are available to instructors and student services personnel interested in incorporating assessment into their career interventions. Further, many of these variables can be assessed using locally developed methods at little to no cost. Careful assessment of career development goals ensures that students are receiving promised services and that the interventions are having the intended results or that steps can be taken to improve outcomes.

References

ACT, Inc. (2008). *Student Readiness Inventory: SRI user's guide.* Iowa City, IA: Author.

ACT, Inc. (2009). *ACT Interest Inventory technical manual.* Iowa City, IA: Author.

Bandura, A. (1986). *Social foundations of thought and action: A social cognitive theory.* Englewood Cliffs, NJ: Prentice Hall.

Betz, N. E., Borgen, F. H., Rottinghaus, P., Paulsen, A., Halper, C. R., & Harmon, L. W. (2003). The Expanded Skills Confidence Inventory: Measuring basic dimensions of vocational activity. *Journal of Vocational Behavior, 62,* 76-100.

Betz, N. E., & Hackett, G. (1983). The relationship of mathematics self-efficacy expectations to the selection of science-based college majors. *Journal of Vocational Behavior, 23,* 329-345.

Betz, N. E., Hammond, M. S., & Multon, K. D. (2005). Reliability and validity of five-level response continua for the career decision self-efficacy scale. *Journal of Career Assessment, 13,* 131-149.

Biggs, D. (1994). *Dictionary of counseling.* Westport, CT: Greenwood Press.

Chartrand, J. M., Robbins, S. B., Morrill, W. H., & Boggs, K. (1990). Development and validation of the Career Factors Inventory. *Journal of Counseling Psychology, 37,* 491-501.

Cole, B., Finch, E., Gowland, C., & Mayo, N. (1995). *Physical rehabilitation outcome measures.* London, UK: Williams and Wilkins.

Crites, J. O., & Savickas, M. L. (1996). Revision of the Career Maturity Inventory. *Journal of Career Assessment, 4,* 131-138.

D'Andrea, M., & Daniels, J. (2001). RESPECTFUL counseling: An integrative model for counselors. In D. Pope-Davis & H. Coleman (Eds.). *The interface of class, culture and gender in counseling* (pp. 417- 466). Thousand Oaks, CA: Sage.

Donnay, D. A. C., Morris, M. L., Schaubhut, N. A., & Thompson, R. C. (2005). *Strong Interest Inventory manual: Research, development, and strategies for interpretation.* Mountain View, CA: CPP Inc.

Fawcett, A. L. (2007). *Principles of assessment and outcome measurement for occupational therapists and physiotherapists: Theory, skills and application.* Hoboken, NJ: John Wiley & Sons.

Gati, I., Krausz, M., & Osipow, S. H. (1996). A taxonomy of difficulties in career decision making. *Journal of Counseling Psychology, 43*, 510-526.

Gay, E. G., Weiss, D. J., Hendel, D. D., Dawis, R. V., & Lofquist, L. H. (1971). *Manual for the Minnesota Importance Questionnaire.* Minneapolis, MN: Vocational Psychology Research.

Goldman, L. (1990). Qualitative assessment. *The Counseling Psychologist, 18*, 205-213.

Gore, P. A., Jr., Brown, S. D., Leuwerke, W. C., & Metz, A. J. (2008). *Student Strengths Inventory technical manual.* Unpublished manuscript.

Gore, P. A., Jr., & Leuwerke, W. C. (2000). Predicting occupational considerations: A comparison of self-efficacy beliefs, outcome expectations, and person-environment congruence. *Journal of Career Assessment, 8*, 237-250.

Heppner, P. P., Wampold, B. E., & Kivlighan, D. M. (2008). *Research design in counseling* (3rd ed.). Belmont, CA: Thomson Brooks/Cole.

Holland, J. L. (1996). *The occupations finder* (4th ed.). Odessa, FL: Psychological Assessment Resources.

Holland, J. L. (1997). *Making vocational choices: A theory of vocational personalities and work environments* (3rd ed.). Odessa, FL: Psychological Assessment Resources.

Holland, J. L., Fritzsche, B. A., & Powell, A. B. (1994). *The Self-Directed Search technical manual.* Odesssa, FL: Psychological Assessment Resources.

Kazdin, A. E. (2003). *Research design in clinical psychology* (4th ed.). Boston, MA: Allyn & Bacon.

Krumboltz, J. D. (1991). *Manual for the Career Beliefs Inventory.* Palo Alto, CA: Consulting Psychologists Press.

Lent, R. W., Brown, S. D., & Hackett, G. (1994). Toward a unifying social cognitive theory of career and academic interest, choice, and performance. *Journal of Vocational Behavior, 45*, 79-122.

Lent, R. W., Brown, S. D., & Larkin, K. C. (1984). Relation of self-efficacy expectations to academic achievement and persistence. *Journal of Counseling Psychology, 33*, 265-269.

Levinson, E. M., Ohler, D. L., Caswell, S., & Kiewra, K. (1998). Six approaches to the assessment of career maturity. *Journal of Counseling & Development, 76*, 475-482.

Neukrug, E. S., & Fawcett, C. R. (2009). *Essentials of testing and assessment: A practical guide to counselors, social workers, and psychologists.* Belmont, CA: Brooks/Cole.

Nevill, D. D., & Super, D. E. (1989). *The Values scale: Theory, application, and research* (2nd ed.). Palo Alto, CA: Consulting Psychologists Press.

Osipow, S. H. (1987). *Manual for the Career Decision Scale.* Odesssa, FL: Psychological Assessment Resources.

Osipow, S. H., & Gati, I. (1998). Construct and concurrent validation of the Career Decision-Making Difficulties Questionnaire. *Journal of Career Assessment, 6*, 347-364.

Sampson, J. P., Peterson, G. W., Lenz, J. G., Reardon, R. C., & Saunders, D. E. (1996). The design and use of a measure of dysfunctional career thoughts among adults, college students, and high school students: The Career Thoughts Inventory. *Journal of Career Assessment, 6*, 115-134.

Sampson, J. P., Reardon, R. C., Jr., Peterson, G. W., & Lenz, J. G. (2004). *Career counseling and services.* Toronto, Canada: Brooks/Cole.

Super, D. E. (1957). *The psychology of careers.* New York, NY: Harper & Row.

Super, D. E. (1983). Assessment in career guidance: Toward truly developmental counseling. *The Personnel and Guidance Journal, 61*, 555-562.

Swanson, J. L., Daniels, K. K., & Tokar, D. M. (1996). Assessing perceptions of career-related barriers: The Career Barriers Inventory. *Journal of Career Assessment, 4*, 219-244.

U.S. Department of Labor, Bureau of Labor Statistics. (2010-2011). *Occupational outlook handbook (OOH).* Retrieved from www.bls.gov/oco

Zytowski, D. G., & Luzzo, D. A. (2002). Developing the Kuder Skills Assessment. *Journal of Career Assessment, 10*, 190-199.

Section II:

Career Programs in the Early College Years

SAINT LOUIS UNIVERSITY

Transitioning Students From High School to College: A Career Development Approach for Deciding Students

Kim Reitter and Leanna Fenneberg

The Institution

Saint Louis University is a private, Jesuit, Catholic university located in St. Louis, Missouri. The University fosters the intellectual and character development of more than 13,313 students in a residential environment, including 8,119 undergraduates. Gender and racial/ethnic demographics are 59% female, 67% White/non-Hispanic, 7% Black/non-Hispanic, 6% Asian/Pacific Islander, 6% nonresident alien, 3% other, 2% Hispanic/Latino, less than 1% American/Alaskan Native, and 8% not specified.

Description of the Initiative

At Saint Louis University, there has been an increase in the number of students entering college still deciding on a major and career. Even those entering with a defined major often shift their intended path during their academic career. A longitudinal study has shown that between 50% and 70% of students will change their major at least once during their academic careers (Gordon & Steele, 2003). Career counseling has been identified as the most efficient intervention to assist students in career planning when compared to either the Strong Interest Inventory or a computer-assisted program alone (Barnes & Herr, 1998). Incoming first-year students experience pressure to declare a major, resulting in anxiety about a career path (Brown & Strange, 1981; Mauer & Gysbers, 1990). Therefore, it is important for students to connect with career services as early as possible in their academic career. While first-year students report an interest in career counseling (Hill & Sedlacek, 1995), many do not pursue this support service, primarily because of the uncertainty about the counseling process (Fouad et al., 2006).

The grounding research in this area, paired with a gradual increase in the number of entering undecided first-year students at Saint Louis University, prompted the development of an early intervention initiative in 2007 for incoming undeclared students. Collaboration between Career Services and Academic Advising resulted in an opportunity for deciding students to meet individually with a career counselor during the two-day summer orientation session. More than 600 students have participated in this early intervention career-counseling program since the initiative's inception. These counseling appointments have proven successful in helping incoming first-year students begin the process of deciding on a major and career.

As academic advisors developed students' individualized schedules for their summer orientation, those who were still deciding on a major were assigned a 30-minute career counseling appointment. Immediately prior to their appointment, students completed the Career Decision-Making Scale, a short assessment designed by the University's Career Services using a 5-point Likert scale to rate career-related statements. The results were used to help the counselor determine the student's areas of need in self-knowledge, career information, career-choice anxiety, and general decision making.

During the 30-minute appointment, the career counselor built rapport and conducted a short intake. The intake, along with the assessment, assisted the counselor in helping students establish up to five goals to complete over the summer. Each student's development plan was individualized around a core of common suggestions, such as talking to professionals in an area of interest, exploring SIGI 3 (i.e., an in-house, computerized interactive assessment tool), researching various web sites containing career information, making a follow-up appointment with the career counselor, and registering for the one-credit hour Career Decision Making course offered and taught by a career counselor during the fall semester.

The career development plan was then copied and placed in a two-pocket folder for the student to take home. Along with the plan, the folder included a calendar of fall Career Services' events, a brochure outlining the menu of available services, a flyer explaining the Career Decision Making course, a pictogram showing the various paths a sample student took to find his calling, directions to access the CareerLink database, a four-year career development plan, and a sheet listing related Internet resources.

Two weeks following the appointment, students received a personalized e-mail message from their career counselor offering continued assistance if needed. Economic and parental pressures facing today's students require them to choose a major and career early during the college experience to ensure an effective four-year curricular plan. Starting the process of career counseling during summer orientation has proven beneficial. While the scope of this specific initiative is the initial meeting during the summer orientation program, other academic advising units have either required or strongly encouraged undeclared advisees to participate in at least one additional career counseling appointment during the first year.

Research Design

Student learning outcomes addressed by this program included values clarification and decision making pertaining to career development. In addition to assessing these outcomes, there was an interest in evaluating students' satisfaction with the career counseling appointment, their intentions to use career services throughout their academic career, and the perceived value of the intake assessment and additional materials given as part of the appointment. To evaluate this early intervention program, two methods of inquiry were used: a summer orientation satisfaction survey and a follow-up career counseling appointment survey.

Summer Orientation Satisfaction Survey

The first evaluative method was a satisfaction survey assessing the overall two-day summer orientation program. Students were asked to rate the various elements of the event, including the career counseling meeting, if attended. This survey was distributed electronically to all participants immediately following the program for the years 2007, 2008, and 2009.

Follow-Up Survey

In 2007, a second assessment was distributed by e-mail at the end of the academic year to the students who participated in the summer orientation career counseling appointments to ascertain the impact the early intervention had on their decision concerning a major and/or career. Using a Likert scale, respondents indicated their level of agreement to eight statements regarding the perceived importance of choosing the right major or career, the levels of stress and confidence in choosing a major and career, and whether or not they would recommend career counseling to other students.

The follow-up survey was not administered in 2008 and was modified and reintroduced as an assessment tool in 2009. A nine-question survey was sent out electronically during the second week of classes. Respondents were asked to rate their degree of understanding of the major/career choosing process and where they were in their decision making as a result of their appointment, as well as the overall helpfulness of the session. The survey also attempted to evaluate the effectiveness of the precounseling assessment, folder information, and career development plan.

Findings

Summer Orientation Satisfaction Survey

Over the three-year period, the summer orientation survey revealed an average 3.4 level of satisfaction (4.0 scale) with the career counselor meeting. While participation in the career counseling sessions is relatively low, the percentage of students meeting with counselors during orientation has increased annually. Response rates to satisfaction surveys average just over 16% (Table 1). Overall, the students who responded to the survey were satisfied with their career counseling appointment (Table 2). Given the low response rates, this finding suggests rather than confirms a pattern of potential impact of the career counseling appointment on students.

Table 1

Overview of Summer Orientation Career Counseling Participation, 2007-2009

Year	Participated in counseling n	%	Responded to survey n	%
2007 ($N = 1,558$)	125	8.02	23	18.40
2008 ($N = 1,445$)	138	9.55	25	18.12
2009 ($N = 1,537$)	188	12.23	24	12.77

Table 2

Student Satisfaction Ratings of Summer Orientation Career Counselor Appointments, 2007-2009

Rating	2007 percentage (n = 23)	2008 percentage (n = 25)	2009 percentage (n = 24)
Excellent	34.78	42.66	41.67
Good	39.13	21.42	37.50
Fair	8.70	7.60	4.17
Poor	0	1.90	0
Did not respond	17.39	26.42	16.66

Students were also asked, "What is the most important thing you learned during SLU 101 [summer orientation program]?" Responses directly related to the career counseling experience included

> It is more than OK that I do not know what my career or major will be. It is important for me to enjoy the college experience while actively pursuing my future.

> The most important thing I learned at SLU 101–my career counselor made a list with me on what I should think of doing later on in life.

> The most important thing I learned at SLU 101 was how to obtain information about majors/careers.

> I really liked talking to the career counselor and my academic advisor. They made me feel better about the fact that I had not decided a major yet.

Follow-Up Survey

Seventeen students (13%) responded to the 2007 follow-up survey, and the majority felt positive about their career counseling experience as evidenced by 12 (71%) deciding on a major by the end of the academic year and 13 (76%) reporting feeling confident or very confident in choosing a major/career. In addition, 11 students (65%) indicated that choosing a major was important or very important to them, and nine (53%) rated selecting the right career path as important or very important. The majority of students also felt their levels of stress regarding a major/career decision had increased by the end of the academic year (and after receiving career counseling) compared to pre-summer-orientation levels: Eight students reported average stress, two indicated high stress, and five rated their stress level as very high. This finding was attributed to the likelihood that career counseling may raise awareness of issues, personal desires and interests, and pending decisions.

Lastly, in rating the value of career counseling, 13 students were likely or very likely to recommend career counseling to their friends.

The modified 2009 follow-up survey was sent to 88 students, and nine (10%) replied. The timing of the survey (one month into the semester) may have contributed to the low return rate. Of the nine respondents, seven agreed or strongly agreed that the counseling appointment was helpful and increased their understanding of the process of choosing a major and/or career. Six students reported that they intended to use career services in the future, and five of these students had already met with their career counselor for a second meeting.

Although the sample sizes for both surveys were small, the combined results suggest that the summer orientation career counseling was beneficial to deciding students in helping them understand the process of choosing a career.

Conclusion

Career counseling appointments for deciding students have become an important component of the two-day summer orientation program at Saint Louis University. This program has helped students initiate career and major decision making before beginning their first year. The assessment methods for the initiative have elicited low student response rates, which inhibit the ability to fully understand program impact. However, the findings suggest that students will find an early 30-minute career counseling appointments helpful and, as a result, may be more inclined to use career services again and recommend career counseling to others.

Minor changes have been made to the program to remedy appointment scheduling problems. Appointments were sometimes set for students who were undecided upon registering for summer orientation but arrived at the event having declared a major. These students reported little benefit from the counseling session. By using an online scheduling system that both advisors and career counselors can access, advisors are now able to make last-minute changes to the schedule to avoid unnecessary appointments.

Future research may include a longitudinal study to see whether students who met with a career counselor during summer orientation changed their major less often and were retained at a higher rate when compared to other students. Another consideration is a more robust pre- and postsurvey for deciding students that will capture contributing aspects of their self-exploration and deciding process and the role that student stress plays in the career decision-making process at various developmental phases. By offering incentives for completing the survey, it is hoped that the response rates will increase and improve the usefulness of the findings.

Key to initiating this type of program at another institution is developing a collaborative relationship and approach between career services and academic advising for scheduling and referral components of the process. A challenge for some campuses may be in the number of students who can feasibly be scheduled during the orientation program. Saint Louis University has five full-time career counselors, however, this program can be replicated at institutions with fewer counselors by using group counseling methods. While individual career counseling allows the counselor to address students' unique needs, group counseling can still provide valuable components.

A final recommendation is to make career services information available to all students participating in summer orientation in order to capture students who are not explicitly defined as undeclared. All students may not need individual career counseling but can benefit from a basic awareness of the resources and services they may use throughout their academic careers as their interests and directions change.

Initiating career counseling to deciding students during summer orientation may help a university promote both the academic and career success of their students. At Saint Louis University, these appointments have helped students begin the process of career decision making prior to starting college.

References

Barnes, J. A., & Herr, E. L. (1998). The effects of interventions on career progress. *Journal of Career Development, 24*(3), 179-193.

Brown, G., & Strange, C. (1981). The relationship of academic major and career choice status to anxiety among college freshmen [Electronic version]. *Journal of Vocational Behavior, 19*(3), 328-334.

Fouad, N., Guillen, A., Harris-Hodge, E., Henry, C., Novakovic, A., Terry, S., & Kantameni, N. (2006). Needs, awareness, and use of career services for college students. *Journal of Career Assessment, 14*(4), 407-420.

Gordon, V. N., & Steele, G. F. (2003). Undecided first-year students: A 25-year longitudinal study *Journal of The First-Year Experience & Students in Transition, 15*(1), 19-38.

Hill, M. D., & Sedlacek, W. E. (1995). Freshman counseling interests. *Journal of The Freshman Year Experience, 7*(1), 27-38.

Mauer, E. B., & Gysbers, N. C. (1990). Identifying career concerns of entering freshmen using my vocational situation. *Career Development Quarterly, 39*(3), 230-239.

NORTH CAROLINA STATE

First Year College: A Major/Career Decision-Making Model for Undecided Students

Carrie McLean, Kim Outing, Donna Burton, and Michelle Crossley

The Institution

North Carolina State University (NC State) is located in Raleigh, North Carolina, near the Research Triangle Park. It is a public, four-year research institution with historic strengths in engineering, agriculture, and technological innovation. With a population of more than 33,819 students (25,255 undergraduate), 8,000 employees, and 2,000 faculty, NC State is the largest university in North Carolina. The student population is 56% male, 73.9% White (non-Hispanic), and 26.1% minority students.

Description of the Initiative

The First Year College (FYC) is one of NC State's 10 academic colleges with a mission to "guide students through a structured process for transition to the University and selection of a major" (First Year College, 2009b). Housed under the Provost's Office in the Division of Undergraduate Academic Programs, FYC annually admits 15-20% (i.e., approximately 800 students) of the incoming first-year cohort who meet highly selective admissions criteria. The FYC is designed for students who choose to take a year to explore majors and careers prior to declaring a major. The three main program goals are

◇ To encourage all FYC students to collaborate with the entire NC State community in order to enhance their own University experience
◇ To encourage students to make an informed and timely decision regarding an academic major and to explore related careers
◇ To help FYC students learn to apply higher-level thinking skills to academic and career decision making

The primary components of the FYC are cross-curricular advising; a residential community (i.e., the FYC Village); and a two-semester, graded, orientation course (one hour per semester: USC 101 and 102). The second program goal is the foundation for the career development initiative embodied in the First Year College.

The strength of the FYC model is the integration of teaching and advising. The advisor of record for a cohort of students is also the cohort's instructor in USC 101 and 102, Introduction to University Education I and II. Through weekly course contact, as well as individual advising appointments, the advisor/instructor comes to know each student's strengths, weaknesses, values, interests, and abilities. That knowledge enables the advisor to better support and facilitate the decision-making process.

During the first semester, FYC students in USC 101 begin to make a successful transition from high school; discover more about themselves and the majors at NC State; and learn how to make a rational, informed decision. In their second semester, the focus on majors and careers expedites the major decision-making process. The career decision-making model employed in the course (Figure 1) is based on self-knowledge, occupational knowledge, and decision-making emphases of traditional career theories. Burton, Brandt, Duhart, Simpson, and Sohns (2009) indicate that this model

> is circular to suggest that decision making is a process. This representation of the model is based on the work of Niles and Hartung (2000). Like a circle, the decision-making process does not have an end-point—even after you decide on a major or a career, you'll find that you'll need to evaluate your decision to see if it fits you as you grow and learn, and as circumstances in college, career, and your personal life change. (p. 2)

FYC students explore various topics, including academic integrity, time management, use of University resources, critical thinking, and diversity awareness. They learn more about themselves through personality assessments, class assignments, and in-class exercises on topics such as goal setting, values, and interests. To explore the majors offered at NC State, students participate in the annual Majors Fair where they have the opportunity to engage with faculty and student representatives from NC State's nine degree-granting colleges. Later in the semester, they research an individual major and gather more detailed information to facilitate their decision making. Additionally, students attend cocurricular programs, career fairs, and information sessions on majors and careers. These programs feature faculty members from different departments speaking about the majors and possible careers in their field, faculty dinner discussions, and faculty cocurricular engagement.

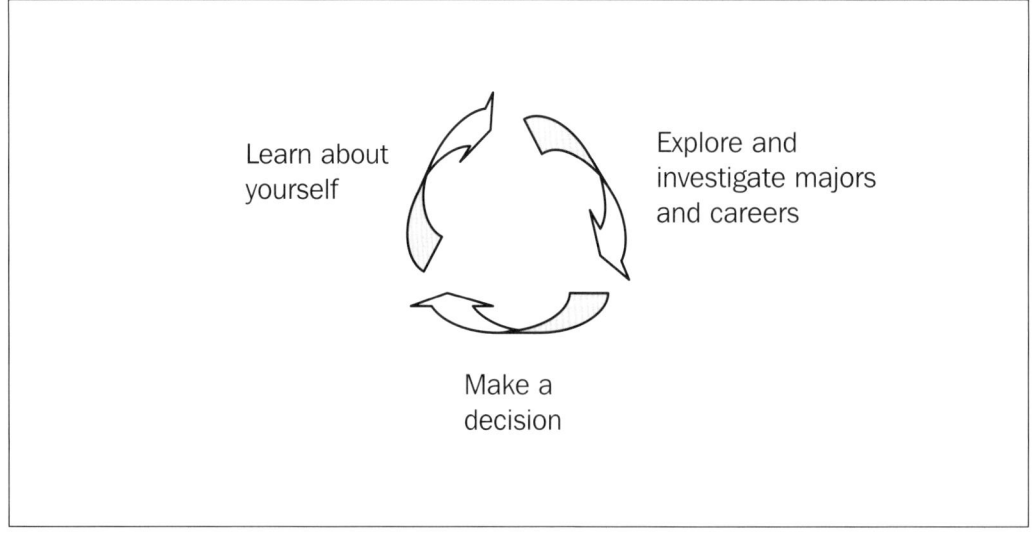

Figure 1: Career decision-making model. Adapted from *Transition to Higher Education Workbook* by D. Burton, S. Brandt, H. Duhart, M. Simpson, and D. Sohns, 2009, p. 2. Copyright 2009 by North Carolina State University. Reprinted with permission.

In USC 102 (second semester), self-exploration continues with assessments that give students a clearer picture of how personality type and interests intersect in career fields that may be satisfying for them. At the Academic Networking event, they interact with upper-class students in majors of interest. As a class assignment, students conduct an informational interview with a person working in a career of interest to them. The final project of the semester is a letter of intent in which the students are asked to describe their decision-making process by discussing the relevance of course activities, career assessments, values, and the relationship to their future work and career goals. The letter of intent can be used as a personal statement for application to majors.

Research Design

The First Year College Assessment Plan is a comprehensive tool used to assess the six broad goals of the program: (a) student engagement, (b) the development of critical thinking skills, (c) diversity awareness, (d) academic success, (e) sound advising, and (f) major and career exploration leading to the informed and timely selection of a major. Each component is critical to the success of the whole initiative and the development of the student. Therefore, while the assessment of major and career exploration will be described here, the other program components play an equally important role in moving the student toward an informed decision.

Several outcomes are related to the major and career exploration and decision-making goal. First, the program is designed to move students from undecided to decided over the course of the first year. Students enter the program at various levels of decidedness, from having no definite ideas about a major to being interested in looking at majors within one or two of the undergraduate colleges. A brief pre-posttest survey on decidedness is used to assess success in meeting this outcome. The pretest is administered prior to the start of the fall semester, during New Student Orientation. The posttest is administered during the last two weeks of the spring semester.

Institutional data have shown that students who fully embrace FYC's goal of major and career exploration are more likely to be retained and perform better academically. This has been confirmed by reviewing data for students who select FYC as their program of choice when they apply to NC State versus students who are admitted to FYC as a second-choice option after they are denied admission to their first-choice program, typically one of the more selective majors at the University. These second-choice students are often closed to the idea of fully exploring the range of possibilities beyond their initial major choice. Committing to the exploration process is one important ingredient to success and satisfaction; therefore, a recent addition to the assessment plan is the evaluation of students' reasons for choosing FYC. To gather this information, comments from the FYC Advising Survey, administered at new student orientation, are reviewed and coded.

Assignments required of FYC students in the first year offer opportunities for self-assessment, information gathering, and more in-depth research of potential majors and careers. Learning outcomes for these activities include broadening one's knowledge of self, majors, and careers, and gaining new information to aid in the evaluation of a specific major or career. These outcomes are assessed through questions in the course evaluation, as well as through evaluations administered for programs such as the FYC Majors Fair and the Academic Networking event.

The FYC course's final project is the letter of intent, which is designed to assess students' decision-making process, and is evaluated using a holistic critical thinking rubric adapted from Facione and Facione (1994). This assignment serves to determine whether students have accurately interpreted evidence from multiple sources, carefully weighed pros and cons, evaluated fit, and come to a sound decision about their choice of major.

Once students have made their decision, the assessment focus turns to matriculating into a major and the successful completion of the degree. Matriculation requirements for that major may include criteria such as GPA, completion of specific courses, and essay application. As part of the FYC course, students must also evaluate their ability to meet matriculation requirements in a timely manner.

Because FYC students are able to take the time needed to make a sound decision on a major, the expectation is that they are likely to be satisfied with their choice, thus reducing major change rates. To assess this, FYC students are compared to their peers who entered directly into a college major (i.e., no FYC experience). Changing majors can often add time to the student's program and negatively impact graduation rates.

As students prepare to graduate, the University-administered Graduating Senior Survey collects information on the overall college experience and future plans. Colleges can elect to include additional questions for their graduates. FYC takes this opportunity to ask students who participated in the program about their satisfaction with their choice of major upon leaving FYC.

Findings

Decidedness

Over the course of the first year, FYC students demonstrate a significant increase in decidedness. For the 2008-2009 assessment, 93% of the FYC entering class of 690 students participated in a pretest survey of decidedness, and 86% of the spring enrollment of 670 students participated in the follow-up posttest survey. For the question, "How close are you to deciding on a major?", students moved from a pretest average of 2.7 to a posttest score of 4.5 on a 5-point decision scale (1 = not close, I'm undecided; 5 = so close, that I've decided), with 90% scoring a 4 or higher.

By the end of the first year, 67% of students indicated that they had decided on a major, and another 19% were considering majors within one college. Ten percent of students were still considering majors within several colleges, and 3% described themselves as undecided, compared to 46% and 25%, respectively, at pretest. These decidedness data are consistent with previous years' assessment findings.

Student feedback frequently identifies class papers, focus group transcripts, the MBTI and Strong Interest Inventory assessments, the career informational interview assignment, and the Majors Fair and Academic Networking programs as having a great impact on their major/career decision process. Learning outcomes for the Majors Fair and Academic Networking were met based on student responses to survey questions after the events. Data from the 2008-2009 academic year revealed 579 students (84% return rate) completed Majors Fair surveys with 97% of the respondents strongly agreeing or agreeing that they learned new information that would be helpful in their major decision process. The Academic Networking survey had a 92% return rate (670 students), and students indicated that the experience increased their understanding of the college or majors they networked with (4.29 on a 5-point scale), that the session content was relevant to their needs at this point in their major/career exploration (4.02 on a 5-point scale), and that they had a better understanding of how the majors related to potential career or graduate school options (4.31 on a 5-point scale).

The letter of intent analysis revealed a need for more critical-thinking practice in the classroom. Although students could articulate where they were in the decision process, they were less competent in identifying their evidence and in constructing their arguments in a formal paper.

Matriculation and Progress

Institutional data have been collected for 15 years comparing major changing and matriculation rates between FYC and non-FYC students. The most recent study analyzing 10 years of data (Donley Educational Evaluation Consulting, Inc., 2006) revealed that approximately 90% of FYC students made no change in their major, once declared. The rate of major change was two to three times greater for the non-FYC cohort ($p < .0001$). FYC students also graduated at rates as high or higher than a matched cohort of their peers who entered the University declaring a major.

Graduating Senior Survey

A total of 479 degrees were conferred in 2007-2008 to students who originated in FYC, and 38% of these students completed an FYC insert in the University Graduating Senior Survey. Reflecting on their FYC experience, 84% of the respondents indicated that FYC prepared them to make an informed choice concerning their major. When asked whether they were satisfied that the major they chose upon leaving FYC was the right major for them, 83% responded positively.

Conclusion

The assessment of the major/career decision-making process in FYC shows that students continue to make expected progress in this area. The data indicate that FYC students learn a significant amount of information about majors and careers and are successful in identifying a possible major or career path during their first college year. Further, the data collected also reflect a 15-year historical trend of FYC students remaining in the major that they have selected during the decision-making process. FYC students continue to outperform a matched cohort of decided University students in terms of grade point average and retention. Both groups have similar graduation rates. The accomplishment of similar graduation rates is particularly impressive given the FYC student has taken a year to explore majors and careers prior to declaring a major.

Although the decidedness results are positive, the FYC Curriculum and Assessment Committees continue to collaborate and conduct further assessment of assignments, programs, and activities related to the major/career decision-making process. While students acquire a wealth of information about majors and careers, participate in a variety of activities and programs, and take several career-related assessments, their ability to synthesize these experiences and articulate how those experiences informed the selection of a major needs some improvement. The curriculum committee has researched critical-thinking skill development and introduced training to help instructors better incorporate critical thinking into class activities and assignments. Critical thinking skills are important as students negotiate not only the major/career decision but also other areas in their lives.

Further qualitative and quantitative assessments are needed to determine the impact of the University's changing intracampus transfer requirements and policy. These intracampus transfer requirements are becoming more and more competitive and sometimes require that FYC students meet a higher academic standard than declared students who are enrolled directly into a major. This makes transferring into a major more difficult for FYC students despite their successful performance and validated commitment to the major. Thus, FYC students may, more frequently than in the past, pursue earlier or immediate transfers in order to obtain necessary courses and minimize the risk associated with waiting longer to transfer. These practices can negatively impact major change rates, satisfaction, and retention. The Assessment Committee is currently considering ways to assess the impact of matriculation policy on transfer timing and choice of a major.

Despite some policy challenges, the major/career decision-making process in the First Year College continues to be successful. The College has been developing and refining its programs for more than 15 years and is committed to continuous improvement. The assessment plan has proven very beneficial to understanding what strategies have best facilitated timely major/career decision making. The FYC assessment process is also adaptable to other institutions interested in developing programs for undecided students. To the extent that program goals are aligned, institutions may review the assessment plan, identify desired outcomes, and use the assessment methods that best meet the needs of their institution (First Year College, 2009a). The success of the major/career decision-making model in the First Year College can be attributed to a strong commitment to assessment and ongoing program improvement; continuous staff development and education regarding career development research, strategies, and activities; and the appropriate identification of students who are committed to exploration, career development, and academic success.

References

Burton, D., Brandt, S., Duhart, H., Simpson, M., & Sohns, D. (2009). *Transition to higher education workbook.* Raleigh, NC: NC State University.

Donley Educational Evaluation Consulting, Inc. (2006). *First Year College 10-year assessment report* (unpublished report). Raleigh, NC: NC State University.

Facione, P. A., & Facione, N. C. (1994). *Holistic critical thinking scoring rubric.* Millbrae, CA: California Academic Press.

First Year College. (2009a, November 2). *Assessment.* Retrieved from NC State University website: http://www.ncsu.edu/fyc/assessment/

First Year College. (2009b, November 2). *FYC's vision and mission statements.* Retrieved from NC State University website: http://www.ncsu.edu/fyc/about/vision_mission.html

CUYAMACA COMMUNITY COLLEGE

CAREER DEVELOPMENT IN A COLLEGE SUCCESS COURSE

Marsha Fralick

The Institution

Cuyamaca College is a public community college located in El Cajon, California. It is a commuter college that offers a variety of programs in vocational education, transfer studies, and courses for personal enrichment. Because the College is located in East San Diego County near the Mexican border and several Native American reservations, it serves many diverse, first-generation, developmental, immigrant, and low-income students. Approximately 9,000 students attend Cuyamaca College; 56% are female, and 40% are over 25 years of age. Many of these students attend part time, which makes the full-time equivalent student enrollment 5,800.

Description of the Initiative

In 1991, Cuyamaca College completed a study (i.e., telephone survey) of a 1,000 students who were enrolled in the fall 1990 semester but failed to re-enroll in spring 1991 to determine their reasons for leaving college. Of these students, 78% considered themselves to be successful because they accomplished their goals (i.e., positive attrition). The remaining 22% were classified as negative attrition since they either did not successfully complete their courses or did not accomplish their goals. When comparing the positive and negative groups, significant differences ($p < .001$) were found in whether or not these students had a definite goal or college major. Students without a defined major or college goal were at high risk of dropping out without achieving success (Fralick, 1993). Based on this research, in 1992 a one-semester, three-unit, college success course with a career development component was designed to improve student retention and success at Cuyamaca College: Personal Development Counseling 124, Lifelong Success (PDC 124).

PDC 124 is built on the foundations of social science and vocational psychology and is taught by faculty with a master's degree in counseling. The course is associate degree applicable and transfers to both the California State University System (CSUC) and the University of California (UC), which has the highest requirements for academic rigor. It is notable that the course transfers as a general education course to the CSUC in Area E, Lifelong Understanding and Self-Development.

The course is recommended for high-risk students who are undecided majors or lack basic skills and moves quickly from theory to practical application. For example, when personality theory is introduced to students, they complete a personality assessment and then apply the theory to their personal lives by exploring majors that match their personality types.

PDC 124 has become part of the culture of the college and has high enrollment. The college offers approximately 50 sections of the course each year, enrolling about 2,000 students in a balance of traditional face-to-face, hybrid, and online formats. It is also offered in 10 local high schools to help juniors and seniors prepare for college and functions as a bridge to aid in successful transition from high school to the community college or university system.

The class is not required, but it is highly recommended by counselors during orientation and counseling sessions, as well as by faculty, to students struggling to be successful in their courses. Because of high enrollment and relatively low cost of the program, the Personal Development Counseling department, which houses the college success course, is one of the top income-producing academic departments in the college.

The demographics of students enrolled in the program match the demographics of the College with two exceptions. Students in the course tend to be younger (i.e., 45% of the students in PDC 124 are less than 20 years old compared to 22% of the general College population) and more diverse (i.e., there is a slightly greater percentage of ethnic minorities enrolled in the course).

The career development component is designed as part of a personal development process in which students explore personality type, learning style, interests, and values. Once students have learned about their personal preferences, they complete career research to match their personal characteristics with the job world, taking into consideration preferred lifestyle, career outlook, and salary information. This component is approximately one third of the course content and is fully integrated into the curriculum.

The theoretical framework for the program is based on personal development and career exploration. Parsons, credited as the father of vocational guidance in the early 1900s (Patton & McMahon, 2006), identified three key elements of career selection:

- Self-understanding, including aptitudes, abilities, interests, and other qualities
- Knowledge of the world of work, including requirements, advantages and disadvantages, career outlook, and compensation
- Matching personal qualities with the world of work

In the course, students embark on the self-understanding component through a four-step process. They begin by exploring personality type using the Do What You Are (DWYA) personality assessment (Tieger & Barron, 2007). The assessment helps them identify their natural gifts and talents as a foundation for self-understanding and career development by assessing personality types based on typical college situations or scenarios. These scenarios are easy to read, and students can readily identify with them.

Personality type is a central theme throughout the course. Once students have their personality assessment results, they gain a deeper understanding of their personality type through journaling and interactive classroom activities. In addition to career decision making, personality type is related to several topics throughout the semester, including learning style, time management, communication, and appreciation of diversity. Personality type influences how students learn, manage their time, and communicate with others who may be different from themselves.

Students continue the process of self-exploration by gaining an understanding of their learning styles and related learning strategies to help them better assimilate new knowledge and become lifelong learners capable of dealing with a rapidly changing world. Students take the Productivity Environmental Preference Survey (PEPS; Price, 2009), a comprehensive inventory that measures preferences in 20 different areas within five categories: (a) perceptual, (b) immediate environment, (c) emotionality, (d) sociological, and (e) physical. The PEPS learning style inventory provides a description of students' learning styles, including a summary of the most important factors affecting their style, and a list of learning strategies helpful in mastering the new and difficult material that students find in college and on the job. Based on survey results, students are able to describe their learning style and list matching learning strategies, which is one of the course outcomes.

An additional goal of the college success course is to help students gain proficiency in the use of technology to enhance student success and career development. Approximately half of the courses are taught using the CollegeScope Student Success Program (2010) in online, hybrid, and some face-to-face courses. This program is an interactive online textbook with integrated career assessments. Students begin the program by taking the DWYA personality assessment and the PEPS learning style inventory. The text is personalized for each student based on the results of these inventories. For example, in the chapter on personality, the student's personality results are included in the chapter. The program includes a student portfolio that contains results of the assessments, online journal entries, and quiz results. Faculty can monitor progress by looking at the online student portfolios and then communicating with students. Faculty are trained in the use of online course management tools (e.g., Blackboard) and post assignments, syllabi, and grades online. The remaining half of the students uses a traditional textbook with online access codes for taking the DWYA and PEPS (Fralick, 2008).

The third step in the self-understanding element is discovering multiple intelligences. Gardner (1983/2003) formulated a more inclusive definition of intelligence and defined it as "the ability to solve problems or to create products that are valued within one or more cultural settings" (p. x). Multiple intelligences include musical, interpersonal, logical-mathematical, spatial, bodily-kinesthetic, linguistic, intrapersonal, and naturalist intelligences. Using a checklist of examples of these multiple intelligences, students examine their abilities and talents. This activity is followed by journal writing on the topic.

Finally, interests and values are considered using Holland's (1973) career development theory, which classifies the basic categories of occupational interests as realistic, investigative, artistic, social, enterprising, and conventional. Interests and related careers in these categories are explored through classroom activities and by matching their interests with occupations listed in *The Occupations Finder* (Holland, 1996). The Choices Planner (XAP Corporation, 2010), which includes the Interest Profiler and Work Values Sorter, is also used to investigate interests, values, and related careers. Lastly, students journal to summarize what they have learned about themselves in this dimension.

Students take advantage of technology to facilitate their exploration of the third element of Parson's model, gaining knowledge of the world of work to match personal qualities to a career or major. The DWYA, PEPS, and Choices Planner are all online assessments that can be accessed any time or any place. Faculty introduce the assessments in class, providing directions, samples, and descriptions of the benefits of doing them. Students then complete the assessments as assignments done outside of the course. Faculty monitor progress by viewing the student online portfolio, which summarizes the assessment results.

Both the DWYA and the Choices Planner lead students to a database of careers, O*Net, developed by the U.S. Bureau of Labor Statistics. Students begin the exploration of the database by researching careers that match their personality types and interests. The online portfolio provides the opportunity to branch out to related careers or to access any career in the database. The database contains information about how the career matches the Holland categories, related occupations and majors, knowledge and skills required, job tasks and activities, and wage information. The Choices Planner also has an extensive database of careers for students to explore based on career clusters or alphabetical order. A list of online career resources is provided, including the *Occupational Outlook Handbook* and the *Occupational Outlook Quarterly*—both published by the Bureau of Labor Statistics (2010; 2010-2011). Toward the end of the semester, students are required to meet with a counselor for career and educational planning and use their career assessment results in this session to assist them in choosing a major and charting their academic course.

Research Design

A program review for PDC 124 was completed in 2005, which included an examination of persistence data provided by Institutional Research. Fall to spring persistence data from fall 2000 to spring 2004 for PDC 124 students were compared to all College students. Data on student success, defined as completing a course with an *A*, *B*, *C*, or *CR* (credit) grade, were also compared between PDC 124 students and all students at the College. As part of the program review in 2005, surveys were administered to a randomly selected sample of 198 students attending classes in spring 2004. They were asked if PDC 124 helped them to choose a career.

Findings

Program review data showed a greater persistence rate for students who successfully complete PDC 124. The average persistence rate from fall 2000 to spring 2004 for the entire College was 57.8 % compared to 85.4% for PDC 124 students.

An analysis of data on student success showed a higher rate of success for those enrolled in PDC 124 as compared to the general population of the College. The average of all student success at the College from fall 1999 to spring 2004 was 65% as compared to 73% for PDC 124 students. Half of the students (52%) completing surveys as part of a program review indicated that the course helped them choose a career. An additional 35% of these students had already chosen a major and were taking the course for personal development or to meet graduation or transfer requirements.

Conclusion

PDC 124, with a strong career development component, has improved student persistence and success at Cuyamaca College and helped students choose a major. While the research findings do not directly link the career component to these improvements, there is a long history of studies documenting the positive effects of career courses in improving student retention and achieving other positive outcomes. Folsom and Reardon (2003) completed a comprehensive survey of the literature on this topic, examining research conducted from 1978 to 2001. These studies show various positive outcomes of career courses, including increased semester-to-semester retention rates; increased college completion rates; increased retention rates for targeted populations, such as female, undecided, and African American students; fewer course withdrawals; and higher graduation rates. Other positive outcomes include improved self-knowledge, positive effects on career development, increased course satisfaction, increased cognitive development, and improved locus of control.

Incorporating career development as part of a college success course has benefits for students, colleges, and society. When students understand their personality types, learning styles, interests, and values, their personal development is enhanced, and they are more prepared to make better choices related to a college major and career. Making informed choices about a major and having clear academic and educational plans help students stay in college and complete their education.

Embedding college success and career development content in social science and vocational psychology courses can facilitate approval of such courses for graduation and transfer. If students receive credit for the course, they are more motivated to enroll. Increased enrollment in courses that enhance student success is financially beneficial to colleges, not only in increased income, but also in increased retention and lower recruitment costs.

Finally, there are many benefits to society. Technology is a powerful tool for career exploration and prepares students for using technology in other college classes as well as in the job world.

Including a comprehensive learning style component in this type of program helps students be successful in college and become lifelong learners who can excel in rapidly changing work and economic conditions. College and career success courses can help institutions achieve their mission of preparing students to be successful citizens who can compete in the global economy.

References

Bureau of Labor Statistics. (2010). *Occupational outlook quarterly*. Retrieved from http://www.bls.gov/opub/ooq/home.htm

Bureau of Labor Statistics. (2010-2011). *Occupational outlook handbook* (2010-2011 ed.). Retrieved from U.S. Department of Labor website: http://www.bls.gov/OCO/

CollegeScope. (2010). *Student success program*. Retrieved from Human eSources website: http://www.humanesources.com/collegescope/index.html

Folsom, B., & Reardon, R. (2003). College career courses: Design and accountability. *Journal of Career Assessment, 11*, 421-450.

Fralick, M. A., (1993). College success: A study of positive and negative attrition. *Community College Review, 20*(5), 29-36.

Fralick, M. A. (2008). *College and career success*. Dubuque, IA: Kendall/Hunt Publishing Company.

Gardner, H. (2003). *Frames of mind: The theory of multiple intelligences*. New York, NY: Basic Books. (Original work published 1983)

Holland, J. L. (1973). *Making vocational choices: A theory of careers*. Englewood Cliffs, NJ: Prentice-Hall.

Holland, J. L. (1996). *The occupations finder*. Odessa, FL: Psychological Assessment Resources.

Patton, W., & McMahon, M. (2006). *Career development and systems theory*. Rotterdam, The Netherlands: Sense Publishers.

Price, G. E. (2009). *Productivity environmental preference survey*. Lawrence, KS: Price Systems.

Tieger, P. D., & Barron, B. (2007). *Do what you are*. New York, NY: Little, Brown, and Company.

XAP Corporation. (2010). *Choices Planner*. Retrieved from Bridges website: http://www.bridges.com/us/prodnserv/choiceplanner_cca/index.html

Florida State University

Career Information-Seeking Behavior: Rediscovering an Effective Career Intervention

Sara C. Bertoch, Robert C. Reardon, Christine Richer, Jill A. Lumsden, and Elizabeth A. Ruff

The Institution

The Florida State University (FSU) is a comprehensive, residential, graduate research university located in Tallahassee on the Florida panhandle. Approximately 30,000 undergraduates and 9,000 graduate students are enrolled annually. The academic organization of the University comprises 15 colleges and 26 major disciplines to satisfy a wide variety of educational interests. Enrollment data from the fall 2008 semester demonstrated that 56% of the student population was comprised of women and that minorities made up 25% with the following breakdown: 43% African American, 43% Hispanic, 13% Asian, and 3% American Indian.

Description of the Initiative

Florida State's first-year seminar, implemented in 1992, was developed to address the issue of retention by integrating students academically and socially into the University environment. Researchers in higher education have theorized that the more students are involved (Astin, 1984) or integrated (Tinto, 1987) into the academic and social fabric of an institution, the more likely they are to succeed. Responding to University and student needs and assessment, the seminar has undergone several modifications since its inception. In the most recent iteration, classes were small, personalized, and highly interactive. Each section was led by an instructional team made up of faculty, staff, graduate students, and undergraduate students who served as instructors, co-instructors, assistant instructors, and peer leaders. The seminar was presented as an optional, one-credit, satisfactory/unsatisfactory-graded course, offered in the fall and summer semesters, and included a career center intervention as a required component of the class.

Between 40 and 70 sections of the first-year seminar (i.e., approximately 1,000 students) visited the Career Center each year. Each section attended a 45-minute standard career presentation that included (a) an overview of what is involved in career choice; (b) an activity linking personal characteristics to occupations and fields of study; (c) details regarding career center services; and (d) a Career Center scavenger hunt, which took place in the Center library. When students first arrived at the Career Center, they were asked to write down three dream occupations. Their responses were recorded on a whiteboard and referenced during the career choice discussion, using a cognitive information processing theory of career development (Sampson, Reardon, Peterson, & Lenz, 2004). During the presentation, students were introduced to Holland's (1997) six RIASEC personality types and asked to pick the three types most characteristic of them. This information was used to identify work environments and fields of study that matched the types. Students then used the *SDS Occupations Finder* (Holland, 2000)—a listing of occupations organized by level of education, training, and Holland code—to locate careers that matched combinations of their three-letter code. Students also identified their major by Holland code using the *Educational Opportunities Finder* (Rosen, Holmberg, & Holland, 1994) and a Career Center handout entitled "Majors by Holland Code."

In addition, students were provided with a brief tutorial describing the many services available at the Career Center (e.g., mock interview program, various career expositions, on-campus interviewing, career portfolio). Lastly, students engaged in a scavenger hunt in the Career Center library to find resources that might be useful for them. The quest included items requiring students to use a computer-assisted career guidance program, locate books pertaining to internships, and take one of 16 modules relating to a career topic of interest.

In exploring additional useful career interventions, FSU recognized the need for developing strategies that draw upon historically effective theory and research, while using current research and media resources that can efficiently reach a wide array of individuals seeking career services. A career intervention derived from this evidence base is model-reinforced learning. The concept of modeling as a learning tool, where learning occurs as a result of watching the behaviors, attitudes, and emotional reactions of others, is based on Bandura's (1969) social learning theory. It was hypothesized that adding a career intervention consisting of a model-reinforced video to the standard presentation would assist students in engaging in more frequent information-seeking behavior and obtaining a wider variety of career information.

Research Design

In the fall of 2008, FSU undertook a pilot study to examine the effects of a model-reinforced learning intervention on the career development of undergraduate students enrolled in the first-year seminar, specifically looking at information-seeking behavior (ISB). The experimental treatment career intervention consisted of a nine-minute video of a student seeking information in the Career Center with the assistance of a career advisor. In the video, a career advisor used verbal and nonverbal cues to reinforce the ISB of a student. Krumboltz and Thoresen (1964) identified six types of ISB (i.e., write, observe, read, listen, visit, and talk) that were reinforced in the video. Fisher, Reardon, and Burck (1976) created a video based on the empirically supported research of Krumboltz and Thoresen and much of the dialogue from that video was used in the development of the experimental video used in this study.

The research design was experimental with a treatment and a control group. Of the 25 first-year seminar sections that visited the Career Center, 12 viewed the video at the beginning of their standard presentation (i.e., treatment) while 13 did not (i.e., control). Students in all sections and both groups were asked to complete three brief (i.e., five minutes to complete) ISB questionnaires sent via e-mail three weeks after the last seminar section visited the Career Center. The measuring instruments included (a) an ISB questionnaire specifically designed for this study, (b) the Career Exploratory Plans or Intentions (CEPI; Betz & Voyten, 1997), and (c) the Career Exploratory Survey-Environmental Exploration (CES-EE; Stumpf, Colarelli, & Hartman, 1983). All three surveys were modified for online use with SurveyMonkey.

Comprised of six questions, the ISB questionnaire (see Appendix A) asked students to report whether, during the fall semester, they had engaged in any career information-seeking strategies based on six action words (i.e., read, write, listen, visit, observe, and talk) and, if they had, how many times and the number of hours they engaged in ISB behavior. For the treatment group, these six action words had been reinforced in the video.

The CEPI is a 5-item self-report inventory designed to measure an individual's intention to perform career decision-making behaviors using a 5-point Likert scale. Sample items include "I intend to spend more time learning about careers than I have been" and "I plan to talk to advisors and counselors in my college about career opportunities for different majors."

The CES-EE is part of the longer Career Exploratory Survey, and the 6-item Environmental Exploration was used to assess career exploratory behaviors of students. Using a 5-point Likert scale, the CES-EE measures "the extent of career exploration regarding occupations, jobs, and organizations within the past semester" (Stumpf et al., 1983, p. 196).

Findings

While the total enrollment of the 25 seminar sections was 537 students, only 27 (5%) students responded to the SurveyMonkey questionnaires, 13 (2.4%) from the treatment group (i.e., viewed the video, however, not all students in the treatment group responded to all questionnaires) and 14 (2.6%) from the control group (i.e., did not view the video). Results from the ISB questionnaire revealed an average of 58% of the respondents in the treatment group had engaged in the six ISB activities, while an average of 33% of the respondents in the control group reported engaging in these six activities.

Table 1 shows that respondents in the control group consistently reported less time spent in information-seeking activities than students in the treatment group. Additional analyses revealed that the 13 students who viewed the video reported 61.9 hours of career information-seeking behavior while the 14 students in the control group spent 13.7 hours in ISB activities, of which the greatest amount was in the talking category.

Table 1

Number of Hours Engaged in Information-Seeking Behavior

	Reading	Writing	Observing	Visiting	Talking	Listening
Treatment	—	12.4	12.3	9.9	14.4	12.9
Control	—	0.4	0.4	1.6	10.1	1.2

Note. Reading not formatted correctly in SurveyMonkey, and results not obtained

Table 2 includes the five CEPI questions and the percentages of respondents from each group who selected either *Agree* or *Strongly Agree* to the question. The results suggest that students who viewed the video intended to engage in career activities at a slightly higher rate than those in the control group on four of the five items (i.e., learning about careers, gaining a better understanding of abilities and interests, obtaining the required education, seeking advisement on majors and careers). The control group indicated a stronger inclination to talk with people about careers.

Table 2

Number of CEPI Respondents Who Agreed or Strongly Agreed to Intending to Engage in ISB

	Treatment (*n* = 12)		Control (*n* = 14)	
	n	%	*n*	%
I intend to spend more time learning about careers than I have been.	9	75.0	5	35.7
I plan to talk to lots of people about careers.	6	50.0	8	57.1
I am committed to learning more about my abilities and interests.	11	91.7	10	71.4
I intend to get all the education I need for my career choice.	11	91.7	12	85.7
I plan to talk to advisors and counselors in my college about career opportunities for different majors.	12	100	10	71.4

The six CES-EE statements and the percentages of respondents from each group who indicated either *More Than Average* or *A Great Deal* on the each statement are displayed in Table 3. Students who watched the video reported more effort to investigate career possibilities and acquire information about specific jobs or companies than those in the control group. In contrast, respondents in the control group focused more on attending various career orientation programs, initiating conversations with knowledgeable persons in their fields, obtaining information on the labor market and job opportunities in their area, and seeking information on specific areas of career interest.

Overall, the results from the three surveys suggest that students who watched the video engaged in more ISB than students who did not watch the video, and students in the treatment group also expressed the intention of spending more time in ISB in the future. For example, they were more inclined to talk with people (e.g., advisors, counselors, workers) about careers, learn more about their abilities and interests, and acquire all the education needed for their career choice. Results were more mixed between the two groups regarding the likelihood of engaging in ISB in their environment as evidenced by the treatment group reporting being more likely to investigate career possibilities or get information about specific jobs or companies, while control group students were more likely to attend various career orientation programs, initiate conversations with knowledgeable persons in their career area, obtain information on the labor market and job opportunities in their area, and seek information on specific areas of career interest.

Table 3

Number of CES-EE Respondents Who Endorsed More Than Average or A Great Deal Responses

	Treatment ($n = 12$)		Control ($n = 14$)	
	n	%	*n*	%
Investigated career possibilities	4	33	4	28.6
Went to various career orientation programs	0	0	4	28.6
Obtained information on specific jobs or companies	2	16.7	1	7.1
Initiated conversations with knowledgeable individuals in my career area	2	16.7	3	21.4
Obtained information on the labor market and general job opportunities in my career area	0	0	1	7.1
Sought information on specific areas of career interest	2	16.7	6	42.9

Conclusion

The procedures used in this study demonstrate how a unit of instruction on career problem solving and decision making could be infused into a first-year seminar and how this instruction might have a positive impact on students' information-seeking behavior. Students in the treatment group may simply have recognized the six action words featured and reinforced in the video presentation and responded more positively to these schema than students in the control group because of a treatment-by-measure interaction that was not controlled in the design of the study. However, the results may provide a measure of the power of the video presentation and reinforcement of the six-action-word schema in increasing ISB.

While the low response rate to the survey was both a surprise and disappointment and limits confidence in the reliability and validity of the results, almost identical numbers of students responded for both the treatment and control conditions, leading to increased confidence in the quality of the results.

Several factors were identified that possibly contributed to the low response rate, including general survey request overload, timing of the survey (e.g., close to a holiday, before the onset of final examinations, too long after the end of the seminar, too short of a period of time to engage and report on ISB), e-mail delivery method (e.g., anecdotal evidence suggests first-year students do not routinely check for university e-mails), and lack of incentives to respond. A further limitation was the failure to capture information relative to reading, perhaps the most important of the six information-seeking behaviors in the ISB questionnaire, which speaks to the issue raised by Shannon, Johnson, Searcy, and Lott (2002) regarding potential problems in transferring survey instruments into web-based systems. Ideally, this study should be replicated in the first-year seminar with improved methodological procedures.

In a related study using this same video, Ruff (2010) examined the effects of video viewing on the general amount of effort put toward engaging in information-seeking activities, the number and variety of career resources used, and career information seeking strategies employed. Participants were 280 undergraduate students enrolled in a career development course and randomly assigned to treatment or control groups. Treatment groups viewed a video modeling a student successfully engaged in career-information seeking behaviors with the assistance of a trained career advisor. Students in treatment groups participated more frequently in behaviors that were explicitly reinforced in the video. Results also demonstrated that the treatment groups spent more hours taking part in a greater variety of ISBs and used more types of career resources.

Taken together, the results of these two recent studies with a video modeling and reinforcing career ISB provide evidence that using such a career information delivery tool can be practical, efficient, and effective in teaching important information-seeking skills. The earlier research reported by Krumboltz and Thoresen (1964) and Fisher et al. (1976) more than 30 years ago may find renewed impact on student learning in the contemporary age of media and information.

References

Astin, A. W. (1984). Student involvement: A developmental theory for higher education. *Journal of College Student Personnel, 25*, 297-808.

Bandura, A. (1969). *Principles of behavior modification.* New York, NY: Holt, Rinehart, & Winston.

Betz, N., & Voyten, K. (1997). Efficacy and outcome expectations influence career exploration and decidedness. *Career Development Quarterly, 46*, 179-189.

Fisher, T. J., Reardon, R. C., & Burck, H. D. (1976). Increasing information-seeking behavior with a model-reinforced video tape. *Journal of Counseling Psychology, 23*, 234-238.

Holland, J. L. (1997). *Making vocational choices.* Odessa, FL: Psychological Assessment Resources.

Holland, J. L. (2000). *The occupations finder.* Odessa, FL: Psychological Assessment Resources.

Krumboltz, J. D., & Thoresen, C. E. (1964). The effect of behavioral counseling in group and individual settings on information-seeking behavior. *Journal of Counseling Psychology, 11*, 324-333.

Rosen, R., Holmberg, K., & Holland, J. (1994). *Educational opportunities finder.* Odessa, FL: Psychological Assessment Resources.

Ruff, E. A. (2010). *The effects of theory-based techniques and media tools on information-seeking behavior* (Unpublished doctoral dissertation). Florida State University, Tallahassee, FL.

Sampson, J. P., Reardon, R. C., Peterson, G. W., & Lenz, J. G. (2004). *Career counseling and services: A cognitive information processing approach.* Pacific Grove, CA: Brooks/Cole.

Shannon, D. M., Johnson, T. E., Searcy, S. A., & Lott A. (2002). Using electronic surveys: Advice from survey professionals. *Practical Assessment, Research & Evaluation, 8*(1). Retrieved from http://PAREonline.net/getvn.asp?v=8&n=1

Stumpf, S. A., Colarelli, S. M., & Hartman, K. (1983). Development of the Career Exploration Survey (CES). *Journal of Vocational Behavior, 22*, 191-226.

Tinto, V. (1987). *Leaving college: Rethinking the causes and cures of student attrition.* Chicago, IL: University of Chicago Press.

Appendix A
ISB Questionnaire

_____   _____
PRINT Name (Last, First)   Date

Directions: We are interested in knowing more about your information-seeking behaviors for educational and career decision making over the past semester. Please read the following directions CAREFULLY and complete each column of this survey:

In the first column, *Engaged in Activity,* **check** the box if you have engaged in that activity in the past semester.

In the second column, *Number of Times,* write the **number** of separate occasions you engaged in that activity over in the past semester.

In the third column, *Total Hours,* write the **number** of hours you spent engaged in that activity over the past semester.

CAREER INFORMATION ACTIVITIES	Check if you have ENGAGED IN ACTIVITIES	Write the NUMBER OF TIMES you have engaged in the activities	Write the TOTAL HOURS engaged in the activities
READ		#	#
WRITE		#	#
OBSERVE		#	#
VISIT		#	#
TALK		#	#
LISTEN		#	#

ENDICOTT COLLEGE

CHARTING A CAREER PATH: THE IMPACT OF REQUIRED FIRST-YEAR INTERNSHIPS

Beverly Dolinsky, Sara E. Quay, and Ashley Serpa

The Institution

Endicott College is a private, residential four-year institution offering master's and bachelor's degree programs in the professional and liberal arts. Located in Beverly, Massachusetts, Endicott provides an education built upon a combination of theory and practice, which is tested through internships and work experience. Nearly 4,200 undergraduate, adult, and graduate students study at Endicott, regionally and internationally. Of the approximately 1,800 undergraduate students enrolled at the College in 2007, 85% were in residence, 60% were female, and 83% returned to continue their studies in 2008. There were 500 first-year students and 50 transfer students in the 2007 cohort.

Description of the Initiative

Since the College's founding 70 years ago, internship experiences have been central to its core educational philosophy. Indeed, Endicott was the first college in the United States to require all students to complete an internship. Today, bachelor's degree candidates complete a sequence of internship courses: two 120-hour, two-credit internships completed during the first and second years, followed by a full-semester 12-credit internship typically completed in the senior year. While each of these three internships plays an important role in the development of the Endicott student, the first-year internship experience establishes a strong foundation for the remaining internships to build upon by allowing students to (a) test their professional and academic interests early in their college education giving them time to explore possibilities, (b) examine their strengths and passions, and (c) acknowledge limitations and misperceptions of a given career.

Research examining the importance of career development within the first year has clearly indicated that opportunities to reflect on one's career aspirations have numerous academic and social benefits. In reviewing the pedagogies most effective for this reflection, written exercises, individualized feedback, information on the world of work, modeling, and building support networks have been found to be critical (Brown et al., 2003; Hildenbrand & Gore, 2005). In examining how often these methods are actually used in first-year seminars, Hildenbrand and Gore found that all but modeling were used by at least 60% of the professors surveyed. The first-year internship experience at Endicott College allows students to engage with all five of these learning opportunities in a powerful and active learning environment. Similarly, the model encompasses both the diverse and specific career exploration processes that Porfeli and Skorikov (2009) claim make a difference in the career development of late adolescents, while encouraging career self-efficacy, which supports stronger vocational identity and engagement (Gushue, Scanlan, Pantzer, & Clarke, 2006). Finally, the internship program under study provides students with the chance to develop their career exploratory skills, a process which might be transferrable to other areas of life (Blustein, 1997).

Required by all incoming first-year students, INT100 Internship I is an exploratory and experiential internship completed in January, between the fall and spring semesters. In preparation for the on-site experience, students begin planning and assignments in the fall semester. Nine learning objectives have been developed for the internship:

- Design and complete a supervised work experience within the chosen field of study
- Develop professional communication skills
- Gain essential job search skills
- Develop learning goals and self-assess the achievement of these goals
- Acquire basic professional competencies
- Gain exposure to professional practices within the chosen field of study
- Explore career options within the chosen field of study
- Gain essential networking skills and professional references
- Communicate, in writing, key accomplishments and learning experiences from the internship

To fulfill these learning objectives, first-year students participate in a pre-internship orientation during the fall semester that meets both online and in person once a month. The pre-internship assignments include the development of a résumé and a target list of potential internship sites. In early December, students submit an Internship Proposal form for approval by their internship coordinator. The coordinator then sends a confirmation letter to the site that describes the program goals as well as the roles and responsibilities of the on-site supervisor, student, and College.

At the start of the internship, the student sets three goals with input from the site supervisor and submits them to the internship coordinator through the College's online platform. During the one-month internship, the student is required to keep a reflective journal and weekly time sheets. Students also have the opportunity to stay connected to their internship coordinator and classmates through an online discussion board. At the conclusion of the internship, the supervisor completes an evaluation assessing six competencies: (a) basic work requirements; (b) ethical awareness and conduct; (c) learning; (d) response to supervision; (e) interactions with clients, customers, and coworkers; and (e) work output.

Upon returning to the College, all students attend group conferences in which leaders and students discuss experiences and field-related trends during the first week of school. Students also complete a five-part reflective paper based on the following areas: (a) the site, environment, and surroundings; (b) the professional's perspective; (c) organizational and individual behavior; (d) transferring and applying learning; and (e) goal attainment. Individual conferences with faculty advisors are held in February where the paper and overall internship experience is reviewed. The advisor completes an open-ended assessment commenting on how well the student's goals were met and the impact the internship had on his or her chosen major and career path. This process allows students the opportunity to reaffirm or shift their academic major and/or career goals.

Research Design

To demonstrate the value of a required first-year internship, a randomly selected sample of students from the 2007 first-year/transfer cohort, who completed a January internship, was examined. The sample consisted of 177 first-year students (i.e., 50% of the cohort) and provided a mixture of professional and liberal arts career interests, an even gender distribution, and a varied student academic profile. Slightly more than half (53%) of the subjects were female. Students were from a range of academic schools: Arts and Sciences (31%), Education (6%), Business and Technology (24%), Communication (6%), Sport Science (20%), and Visual and Performing Arts (13%). Reflecting the diversity of academic programs, students completed internships in a variety of settings: business (39%), medical (5%), educational (29%), legal (9%), nonprofit (5%), research (1%), and other (12%). The research design included archival analysis of the following assessment measures:

- *Students' three-goal worksheets*. Goals were recorded and coded using a 3-point scale as to whether the goals were met (i.e., 1 = goal not met, 2 = goal partially met, 3 = goal met).
- *On-site supervisor evaluations*. A 5-point Likert scale was used to rate the student in each of the six competency areas (i.e., 1 = unacceptable to 5 = excellent).
- *Internship papers*. In addition to the five reflection areas, students were asked to respond to three questions:
  - How did specific college courses and learned concepts help you prepare for the internship? Qualitative responses were coded numerically on a 7-point scale: 1 = no connection to 7 = strong connection.
  - How did the career-related information you gained in this internship change (or confirm) your future academic plans, internship plans, or career plans? Qualitative responses were coded numerically on a 2-point scale: 1 = changed plans and 2 = confirmed plans.
  - How will you apply what you learned in this internship to different areas of your life (jobs social situations, community service, classes)? Qualitative responses were coded and analyzed for themes.
- *Faculty/student internship conference sheets*. Completed by faculty advisors during the postinternship meeting, faculty advisors wrote their responses to the following prompts: How has this internship experience affected the student's academic and career goals? and Did the student leave the experience with ideas for their next internship experience?

Each specific objective result was recorded using an Excel spreadsheet. The quantitative data were analyzed using SPSS statistical software. For the open-ended qualitative data, all responses were read and transcribed on the spreadsheet. Relevant text was first identified, and repeating themes were classified and color coded. The frequency of responses in each theme were counted and recorded as percentages.

Findings

Of the 177 students, 88% said that they met all three of their internship goals. Seven percent reported that they partially met one or more of their goals, while 2% claimed that they did not meet one or more goals.

On-site supervisors rated the majority of students as *excellent* (i.e., 5 on the 5-point scale) in all six competencies: basic work skills (84%); ethical awareness and conduct (78%); learning (75%); supervision (71%); interactions with clients, customers, and coworkers (64%); and work output (71%).

Eighty-nine percent of the students reported that their internship confirmed their academic/career goals, while 6% of students claimed their experience changed their plans. When analyzing students' reflections on the impact of their internship, the primary theme focused on how the internship helped them gain a better understanding of the options within the career path they were exploring and confirm or change a major, as summarized by these student comments:

> My internship will highly assist me in narrowing down the field that I would like to study in psychology.

> My internship experience was absolutely amazing and entirely beneficial to me because it confirmed my interest in becoming a classroom teacher. Before Christmas break, I still wasn't sure that education was where I wanted to be. After my internship, I am entirely sure that education is where I want to be and where I am meant to be.

In addition to learning more about their chosen career, a second theme in the data pertained to the development of intra- and interpersonal skills as a result of their internship. Seventeen percent reported their internship enhanced their personal strengths and qualities; made them aware of areas needing improvement; allowed them to develop better interpersonal interactions with others; or gave them perspective on how their experience could be generalized across situations, careers, and life experiences. The following student responses reflect this theme:

> Previous to the internship, I was very shy and tentative to talk to people and discuss my opinions. By the end of the 120 hours, I took to answering the phones and talking to clients without worrying about what to say.

> I think that my weakness is that sometimes I lack the ability to direct myself in my work....I think I need to learn to gain more confidence in what I do to become more successful.

> This internship has provided me with the strength to be a more independent person and make better decisions for myself.

> What I realized after my internship was over was that there is one class that you cannot take in college. You cannot be taught how to deal with people, you can only develop these skills on your own.

> I will apply the skills I learned from the internship in all aspects of my life. From organizational skills to communication skills, I feel like I gained a lot to be used in my professional and academic life.

A third theme reflected students' ability to make connections with their academic coursework. Seventy-six percent of the students said that there was a connection or strong connection to their classes. More specifically, as demonstrated in the comments below, students found that the internship experience helped them (a) understand their internship site, (b) understand the material they had studied during the semester, (c) achieve greater success in the college classroom, and (d) become more motivated to work hard.

> I can now see why going to college prepares you for the outside world.

> I was able to apply my criminal justice class to my internship many times. In every capacity of my internship, I was familiar with most of the terminology and processes.

This internship mainly pulled my scattered thoughts on the subject together.

This internship will help me manage my time better, therefore, having a positive effect on my grades.

Conclusion

Endicott College's required first-year internship program is a successful model for providing effective career development tools to new college students. The experiential learning opportunity enables students to meet the course's nine learning objectives. The findings clearly demonstrate the benefits when entering students explore their career paths through a first-year internship. The opportunity helps to confirm students' career choices and narrow options within the disciplines. The internship provides insight into a student's interpersonal strengths and weaknesses and allows students to perceive the value of their college classroom education. Finally, the experience increases the motivation for students to persist in their scholarly activities.

There is a significant amount of work involved by many individuals to assess this program; however, the value to the student and institution clearly supports the effort. After completing this project, it has become clear that findings should be shared with current and future students as well as other stakeholders. Current students may benefit from hearing about the experience of other students, making them more alert to opportunities for learning—both academic and personal—during the internship. Finding out about the value of internships might also encourage future students to think more deliberately about their internship sites and goals. Faculty may choose to refine their pedagogy to make more explicit connections between classroom learning and students' internship experiences, thereby reinforcing the relationship between the two. Finally, internship data documentation can demonstrate to administrators and trustees that the internship program contributes to the fulfillment of the College's mission. In addition to disseminating the findings to these stakeholders, the research could be furthered by assessing the impact of the second-year internship as well as the full-semester senior-year internship.

For institutions wishing to implement a similar program, it is recommended that students receive academic credit for their internship, which could be offered either during winter break or in the summer. Endicott's experience has indicated the internship is of greater value if it is at least 35 hours per week at a single site over a shorter period (i.e., minimum of three weeks) rather than part-time spread out over a longer period or over multiple sites. To ensure students are doing more than office paperwork or answering phones, internship sites need to be approved beforehand. Lastly, obtaining data from on-site supervisors, faculty advisors, and the students affords a comprehensive and holistic evaluation of the program's benefits, strengths, and weaknesses.

References

Blustein, D. L. (1997, March). A context-rich perspective of career exploration across the life roles. *The Career Development Quarterly, 45*(3), 260-274.

Brown, S. D., Ryan Krane, N. E., Brecheisen, J., Castelino, P., Budisin, I., Miller, M., & Edens, L. (2003). Critical ingredients of career choice interventions: More analyses and new hypotheses. *Journal of Vocational Behavior, 62*, 411-428.

Gushue, G. V., Scanlan, K. R. L., Pantzer, K. M., & Clarke, C. P. (2006). The relationship of career decision-making self-efficacy, vocational identity, and career exploration behavior in African American high school students. *Journal of Career Development, 33*(1), 19-28.

Hildenbrand, M., & Gore, P. A., Jr., (2005). Career development in the first-year seminar: Best practice versus actual practice. In P. A. Gore, Jr. (Ed.), *Facilitating the career development of students in transition* (Monograph No. 43, pp. 45-59). Columbia, SC: University of South Carolina, National Resource Center for The First-Year Experience and Students in Transition.

Porfeli, E. J., & Skorikov, V. B. (2009). Specific and diversive career exploration during late adolescence. *Journal of Career Assessment, 18*(1), 46-58.

GETTYSBURG COLLEGE

A Modern-Day Apprenticeship Program
Julie Neill

The Institution

Founded in 1832, Gettysburg College, in Gettysburg, Pennsylvania, is a private, four-year, co-educational, residential college of approximately 2,600 students from more than 40 states and 35 countries. Ranked consistently in the top tier of the nation's liberal arts colleges, Gettysburg engages students in a comprehensive educational experience that is distinguished by a commitment to integrated learning inside and outside the classroom. The student population is 48% male, 82% White, 4% Black, 1% Asian or Pacific Islander, 3% Hispanic, and 2% nonresident aliens.

Description of the Initiative

Since the summer of 2005, the College's Center for Career Development has run a highly successful externship program. This unique career immersion program provides week-long intensive, job-shadowing experiences with alumni and parent mentors. While the program has grown and evolved over the years, the one aspect that has remained constant is the positive impact the program has had on its participants. Students are often surprised by how much they are able to learn in a short period of time. Many come away from the experience with a fresh perspective about their future careers and career-related issues, and the experience often serves as a motivational springboard inspiring students to pursue internships and additional career-related experiences.

The goals of the externship program include (a) helping students gain a realistic understanding of a particular career, including assessing how good a fit that career might be based on their skill set, values, and personality and (b) assisting with students' overall career exploration processes and professional development. While students of all class years are able to participate, first-year students and sophomores are especially encouraged to apply. A total of 136 students have participated in the program since its inception.

Each externship is unique and may be structured somewhat differently. However, externship hosts are encouraged to incorporate students into a variety of activities (e.g., meetings, special events, conference calls, client visits) to enhance their career exposure and to provide students with the opportunity to meet different people within the organization representing a range of job functions. Creating a short-term project for the student to work on during the externship is also strongly recommended.

To foster the mentoring relationship between host and extern, a key component of the program, externship hosts provide home stays, when possible, for students during the week. Home stays enable the pair to engage in after-hours discussions and allow the student to gain a better understanding about work/life balance issues in order to assess a career in a more holistic fashion.

For example, students paired with hosts who are working mothers often comment on having gained a very realistic understanding of the challenges of juggling parenthood with their careers.

To apply, students must submit their résumé and complete a number of short-answer questions concerning their career interests and goals, as well as brief explanations for their site choices. Each application is read carefully to determine the best fit between student and host. To maintain equal access, all students are eligible to receive financial assistance for externship expenses.

Rigorous assignments are required throughout the entire process to ensure the student is appropriately prepared for the experience and maintains a high-level of engagement. Each extern is assigned a career counselor who serves as a liaison and helps guide the student through the experience. Prior to the externship, students must establish learning goals and research the company and industry in which they will be working to ensure at least a basic knowledge of the organization's work.

During the externship, students post blog entries based on guided reflection questions for each day. The career counselor liaison monitors the posts and responds as necessary, providing advice and/or encouragement. To build on networking skills, externs are encouraged to set up informational interviews with other staff members at the organization. At the end of the experience, students complete a reflective evaluation, write a thank you note to their host, and produce a creative assignment.

While the externship itself may only last a week, the entire experience does not end there. Students are strongly encouraged to maintain contact with their host and any other networking contacts they established during the externship. They are also encouraged to arrange a follow-up meeting with their career counselor liaison to assist them with determining next steps. Finally, students are asked to share their experience with the campus community (e.g., give a presentation, serve as a panelist for a special event, or write an article for a campus publication).

As Hildenbrand and Gore (2005) point out, "A growing number of authors argue that environmental exploration is a strong predictor of positive career outcomes" (p. 49). Externships provide students with an insider's look into a specific career field and hands-on, real-world experience. Moreover, the program is structured to incorporate four of the five components that Brown and Ryan Krane (2000) identified as being critical to the success of a career intervention (i.e., written exercises, information on the world of work, modeling, and attention to building support). As mentioned earlier, the mentoring relationship between host and extern is a key component of the program. It is also significant that almost all hosts are either alumni or parents of current students. As a result, externs are often able to relate to their hosts more easily and, in some cases, draw parallels between themselves and their hosts.

Research Design

From 2005-2008, students were asked to complete a primarily qualitative evaluation form. However in 2009, the evaluation form was revised to better assess learning outcomes and includes six open-ended questions, five learning outcome questions and several questions related to administrative aspects of the program. The self-assessment questions ask students to assess their skills and abilities prior to and following the externship experience on a 5-point Likert scale. The open-ended questions are designed to help students reflect on the impact of the experience on their career exploration, including whether or not they are still considering this particular field.

The main objectives of the evaluation are to determine how the externship experience influenced the student's career exploration process and to assess the program's impact on students'

- ◇ Understanding of career interests and goals
- ◇ Networking skills
- ◇ Knowledge of skills required for success in career field of externship
- ◇ Ability to assess fit between personal traits and career in field of externship
- ◇ Awareness of how personal background and experiences impact career choice

In addition to the individual student evaluations, an informal debriefing session is held to elicit student feedback and to allow students to reflect on their experiences with other participants and their career counselor liaisons. Finally, externship hosts also complete evaluations to gather their feedback on the program and their student externs. Hosts are specifically asked to comment on their student's preparedness for the externship, communication skills, interpersonal skills, and overall work performance. This information is used to indirectly assess how well the program prepared participants.

Findings

Thirty-nine students participated in externships in 2009, and all 39 students completed the revised evaluation form, which included quantitative measures. The means for each of the five self-assessment measures (i.e., prior to and following the externship) were calculated, and students perceived that they improved on all of the test variables (Table 1). A paired sample t-test found statistically significant improvement ($p < 0.001$).

Table 1

Self-Assessment of Learning Outcomes

Learning Outcome	Rating of skill level	Mean	N	SD	Std. error mean
Understanding of my career interests and goals	Prior to externship	3.28	39	.857	.137
	After externship	4.31	39	.655	.105
Networking skills	Prior to externship	3.05	39	.826	.132
	After externship	3.95	39	.647	.104
Knowledge of skills required for success in career field of externship	Prior to externship	3.03	39	.903	.145
	After externship	4.33	39	.662	.106
Ability to assess the fit between my personal traits and a career in field of externship	Prior to externship	3.21	39	.951	.152
	After externship	4.44	39	.552	.088
Awareness of how my personal background and experiences impact my career choice	Prior to externship	3.41	39	.993	.159
	After externship	4.41	39	.677	.108

The externship experience yielded clear benefits with regard to students' career exploration process. The majority of students (82%) rated their overall experience as *excellent*, with many describing their experience as invaluable:

I cannot reinforce enough how beneficial I think externships are. It is a week where you can really see the inside of a certain career and understand relatively quickly whether the site is a good fit for you or not. Between my two externships and internships, I think I have saved myself years of dead-end careers. (Senior, political science and English double major)

I achieved more than I thought I ever could. I learned so much about the career, the lifestyle, science, how to network, how to interact with patients, what I should be doing to prepare for a career in medicine, a lot about the oncology specialty along with other specialties, etc. The list goes on and on. (Sophomore, biochemistry major)

I've learned more there about the real world in just a week than I have learned in the two years that I've been in college. The externship has completely changed my attitude about school, and now I can see how the things I have learned in school are applied to the real world. (Sophomore, economics major and international student)

I think I got more out of the program than I ever expected to, and it truly helped me gauge what type of career I am most interested in. (Sophomore, economics major)

My externship…was an unforgettable experience that I believe will really help to shape my future path and career.… I can honestly say that from my early morning start until the time the office fell empty at night, I never once felt bored or even tired; I was so excited to absorb what was happening all around me that I never thought much of anything else. (First-year student)

This was a life changing experience for me. (Sophomore, management major)

In addition, anecdotal evidence suggests past externship participants tend to use the College's Center for Career Development services and participate in experiential learning opportunities at higher rates.

Conclusion

The externship program requires a considerable amount of administrative effort to ensure success. Institutions wanting to implement this program will need to make a significant commitment in terms of staff time. Good communication between career center staff and hosts is also essential. The initiative's success is in large part due to the hosts' ability and desire to mentor students and their creative thinking and planning to design an immersive introduction to a career field. Another important component is the adequate preparation of the students for their externship experience, including logistical information and basic networking and office etiquette skills.

As the program evolves, the following recommendations have been made to improve the evaluation and assessment process:

- Develop a more efficient data tracking system
- Add a self-assessment question related to a student's drive to pursue other career-related activities (e.g., internships) to better evaluate student's motivation levels
- Investigate the longer-term effects the program has on participants by conducting follow-up evaluations with participants one to three years postexternship

With a solid foundation and clear direction for future improvement, Gettysburg College's externship program has established itself as an effective and successful career development initiative.

References

Brown, S. D., & Ryan Krane, N. E. (2000). Four (or five) sessions and a cloud of dust: Old assumptions and new observations about career counseling. In S. D. Brown & R. W. Lent (Eds.), *Handbook of counseling psychology* (3rd ed., pp. 740-766). New York, NY: Wiley.

Hildenbrand, M., & Gore, P. A., Jr. (2005). Career development in first year seminars: Current practice versus best practice. In P. A. Gore, Jr. (Ed.), *Facilitating the career development of students in transition* (Monograph No. 43, pp. 45-59). Columbia, SC: University of South Carolina, National Resource Center for The First-Year Experience and Students in Transition.

Elon University

Charting Your Journey: Life Entrepreneurs Program

Catherine King, Alexa Darby, and Christopher Gergen

The Institution

Elon University in Elon, North Carolina, is a master's-level private university with approximately 5,000 full-time undergraduate students and 343 full-time faculty members. The students are traditional-aged, 81% White, and 59% female. With a strong liberal arts core and preprofessional schools in communications, business, and education, Elon emphasizes engaged learning both in the classroom and through study abroad, undergraduate research, internships, and service-learning.

Description of the Initiative

Baxter Magolda (2002) has called on colleges to better prepare students to be the authors of their own lives. Based on a longitudinal study that followed a cohort of college students through young adulthood, Baxter Magolda (2001) stressed the need to assist young adults in developing an internal compass with which to navigate life's journey. Responding to similar calls from alumni, parents, and community business partners, Elon University developed a Life Entrepreneurs program to train students to be flexible, adaptable, and willing to take risks in order to succeed in a globally competitive, rapidly changing world.

The Charting Your Journey: Life Entrepreneurs Program, designed by leadership developers Gergen and Vanourek (2008) and coordinated through the Office of Student Life, has a focus on cultivating a capacity for self-authorship (i.e., Baxter Magolda's internal compass); imagining possibilities; exploring resources; and creating and committing to a plan for achieving educational, professional, and personal goals (Savickas et al., 2009). It is targeted to sophomores, who confronted with the task of declaring major, may be at a more critical transition point in aligning their personal and professional goals with their core identity. Sophomores can also experience a second-year slump as their initial enthusiasm for college wanes in the face of the need to set goals for the future. Where first-year students may see only opportunities, sophomores begin to see obstacles, especially in the form of negotiating a resolution between their own desires, the expectations of others in their lives, and the available resources (Swanson & Tokar, 1991). Building students' confidence in their own ability to make decisions and act on them can enhance their capacity to explore a wider range of future possibilities for themselves (Blustein, 1989).

In 2009, 32 Elon University sophomores (i.e., both transfer and nontransfer) participated in a pilot of the Life Entrepreneurs program. Students were recruited though e-mails and word-of-mouth and were selected based on their stated interest in guidance for developing a short- and long-term personal and professional life plan and in being part of a peer group to accomplish this goal. There was no extra cost to the students as the funding for program came from the Office of Student Life.

Participants were divided into three cohorts, each co-led by a faculty or staff member and an upper-class peer leader trained by professional facilitators. The group participated in a three-day retreat before the winter term in the nearby Blue Ridge Mountains. *Life Entrepreneurs: Ordinary People Creating Extraordinary Lives* (Gergen & Vanourek, 2008) was used as a text with a supporting workbook created for the program by the same authors. The retreat introduced the core topics (i.e., exploring identity, recognizing opportunities, and developing a vision for the future) through a large-group lecture and activities (e.g., constructing a visual autobiography, teambuilding tasks), while also providing opportunities for individual reflection and small group discussion.

The program was designed to challenge students to think intentionally and purposefully about who they are, where they want to go, and how to get there. This included helping students identify their strengths and passions, explore new opportunities, develop a vision for their future, set goals, craft an action plan, and practice the art of reflection and renewal. By the retreat's end, each student created a personalized entrepreneurial life plan. Following the retreat, the participants met in cohorts weekly during winter term to maintain a high level of peer support as they further reflected on their path and discussed the progress of their plan. They continued to meet weekly throughout the first half of the spring semester as part of a six-week, one-credit Transition Strategies course, taught by the cohort leaders and designed to reinforce the importance of life planning and life entrepreneurship. Students were provided guidance in operationalizing and refining the action plans they had created during the retreat.

Research Design

Students who participated in the pilot were interviewed by two faculty members before and after the program to assess the initiative's impact on their sense of self and plans for the future. The first interview, with 32 students, began with an open-ended format to establish rapport and elicit the participants' reasons for signing up for the program. The main focus of the interview was the participants' sense of themselves. Based on the work of Abes and Jones (2004), students were asked to generate a list of labels that described themselves and map those labels onto a Multiple Dimensions of Identity model (Jones & McEwen, 2000; see Figure 1). This model depicts a core sense of self surrounded by intersecting rings, or identity dimensions, which may include roles, vocation or vocational goals, ethnicity, sexuality, religion, political ideology, and any other characteristic an individual recognizes as an essential part of his or her identity. According to Abes and Jones, at different times and in different contexts, certain aspects are more salient than others. For example, during a religious holiday a student's spirituality may be more salient, while on the soccer field her sense of herself as an athlete may be more prominent.

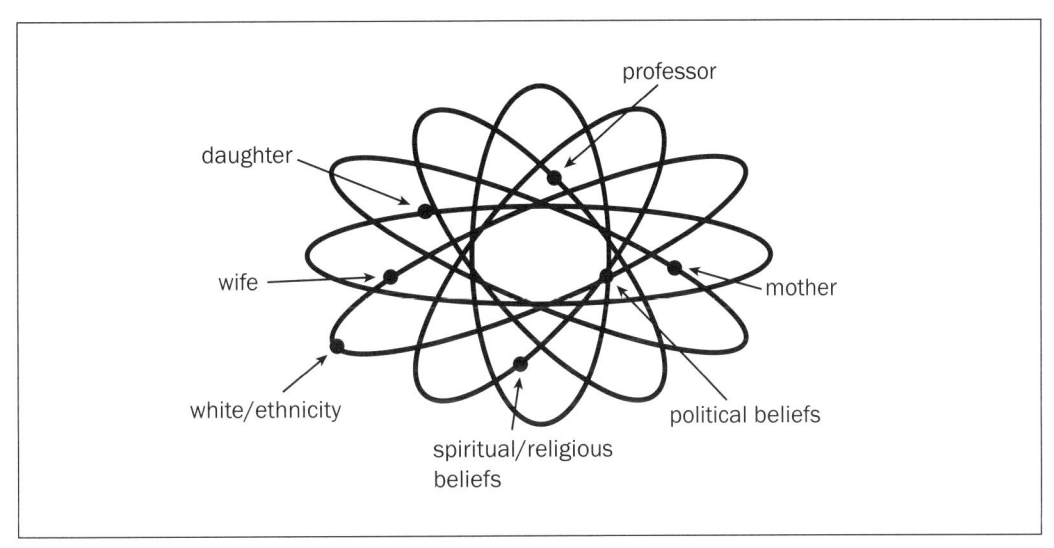

Figure 1. An example of a Multiple Dimensions of Identity model. Adapted from "A Conceptual Model of Multiple Dimensions of Identity," by S. R. Jones and M. K. McEwen, 2000, *Journal of College Student Development, 41,* p. 409. Copyright 2000 by ACPA Publishing. Reprinted with permission.

The Multiple Dimensions of Identity model assumes that young adults gradually develop a capacity for making meaning that is more abstract and complex than that of adolescents (Perry, 1968). Jones and her colleagues (Abes, & Jones, 2004; Abes, Jones, & McEwen, 2007) contend that this meaning-making capacity extends to the self, so that as young adults gain maturity and experience, they become increasingly able to integrate previously disparate components of themselves. At the same time, they become better able to filter external influences so their sense of self, their values, and their plans for their lives become more internally based.

Students were also asked to reflect on whether any facet of their identity had recently become more or less salient and to describe any conflicts they might be experiencing between aspects of themselves. Students described how they attempted to negotiate these conflicts. Their responses provided a sense of whether and how students are able to integrate multiple aspects of identity and balance internally defined goals, beliefs, and values with others' expectations to determine their actions (Pizzolato, 2005).

The follow-up interviews focused on the students' experience in the Life Entrepreneurs program. Twenty-nine participants were interviewed at this time; two participants had not completed the program and one did not come to her second interview. Students were asked to relate what happened during the retreat, what they thought about the text, and how the course had been organized. They also provided feedback on how the program had influenced their view of themselves, their plans for their remaining time in college, and their future goals after graduation. Participants reviewed their Multiple Dimensions of Identity models from the initial interview and were asked how they may have changed (e.g., elements that may have moved closer to or further from their core, any conflicts they were experiencing at the present time and how they were negotiated).

The interviews were transcribed and analyzed using constant comparison, a grounded theory methodology (Glaser & Strauss, 1967). Transcriptions were coded according to statements that reflect the meaning participants attached to their experiences. When patterns across interviews were found, the statements were grouped into categories and themes. As themes were identified, the raw data were re-examined, guided by the new interpretations. This method provided information on both the meaning participants made as individuals and common patterns of meaning making across the group of students.

Findings

When interviewed at the end of the program, participants were highly enthusiastic, particularly about the retreat. The mountain setting emphasized the special nature of the time apart from their everyday lives. The Life Entrepreneurs text and the presence of co-author Christopher Gergen were both engaging and motivating, emphasizing that students had the potential to chart their own journeys. The small- and large-group activities helped them clarify their values and strengths and explore ways to integrate their passions into their goals for the future. The small-group activities provided an intimate and supportive setting for honest examination of their lives.

How students described the changes in themselves and their current activities as a function of their experience in the program was of particular interest. Four themes were identified: (a) increased motivation to make the most of their remaining time in college, especially by focusing on activities related to their goals for the future; (b) increased desire to integrate their passions and interests into their plans for the future; (c) increased willingness to take risks in either social or academic venues; and (d) an increased focus on their interpersonal relationships.

Overall the program, including the Life Entrepreneurs text, helped participants to see that they can take an active rather than passive role in their own transition to adulthood. As one participant observed:

> It's just basically all the dreams and the goals that you have became an action plan you could actually see and make decisions . . . And so it forced me to just grab a hold of all the stuff I've been ranting or complaining or dreaming about and actually point it in a certain direction and take a step forward. It was really good. I loved it.

The Multiple Dimensions of Identity model exercise and follow-up question provided feedback on participants' progress toward self-authorship and how they negotiated multiple perspectives or conflicts. The most frequently reported type of conflict (Table 1) involved the expectations of others: Participants often reported that their friends or parents expected certain things from them that differed from what they wanted for themselves. Many conflicts were related to lack of time for all their activities, especially balancing the demands of the student role and the desire have an active social life, work on or off campus, or pursue personal activities and passions. Of note are the two categories that students did not report before the program, but which several identified after the program: (a) existential issues (e.g., Can I be a moral person and not be religious?) and (b) no conflict. This finding may reflect the students' continuing and multilayered journey toward a deeper exploration and understanding of self.

Table 1

Reported Student Conflicts and Negotiating Strategies (N = 29)

Nature of conflict	Before program	After program
Expectations of others	22	8
Time for activities, roles	17	11
Passions	1	2
Existential issues	0	4
No conflict reported	0	5
Negotiating strategies		
No strategy - conflict not resolved	13	7
Pick one perspective, exclude other	8	2
Compromise between two perspectives	9	4
Reframe issues to eliminate sense of conflict	5	17

Note. Only data from students who completed both interviews were used.

The total number of reported conflicts decreased from the initial interview to the follow-up interview, and there was a noticeable shift in the strategies participants reported using to deal with the conflicts. Prior to the program, participants most frequently indicated that ongoing conflicts were not resolvable or that the only resolution was to compromise or pick one perspective over another. Following the program, students frequently referred to lessons they had learned through the program to describe their efforts to reframe the conflicts in their lives. For example, one student realized that she could satisfy her parents' expectations as well as her own dreams by pursuing a career that combined her love of fashion with her major in business:

> It made me think what I want to do versus what my parents want me to do. The majority of my life I've tried to please my parents and then I have this constant battle with myself. The program has helped me identify what I'm really interested in. I want to see what internships I can have this summer and next summer. I'm hoping to get an internship in the business marketing aspect of a fashion industry. Because I'm really interested in fashion and if I can use my major to my advantage in an industry that I'm very interested in then I feel like I would have definitely gotten out of my major what I wanted.

Conclusion

The Charting Your Journey: Life Entrepreneurs Program clearly responds to Baxter Magolda's (2002) call to better prepare college students for their own developmental journey. The initiative provides young adults an opportunity to question; reflect; clarify goals and values; and develop new, more powerful ways of making meaning in their lives as a basis for action. The participants described the program's impact on their motivation to focus on high-priority activities, their efforts to align current activities with their plans for the future, their willingness to take academic and social risks, and their valuing of interpersonal relationships. The shifts in the students' descriptions of their strategies for negotiating conflict between differing roles, responsibilities, passions, and expectations reflect a growing ability to construct their own identity, goals, and values through an intentional integration of their own desires and the reasonable demands of important others in their lives.

Building on the success of the first year of the program, Elon has worked to simultaneously expand the program and reduce its costs per student to the University. In 2010, four cohorts of 10 to 12 students participated in the program, including a group of first-year students in the Leadership Program. The retreat was held closer to campus and did not include an overnight component. A similar evaluation plan is being used. Students will be interviewed before and after their participation in the program, but a more structured protocol will be implemented, with prompts drawn from the categories derived from the previous open coding of interview data. The more structured format will make it easier for undergraduate research students to conduct the interviews with greater validity. In addition, a third interview during the spring semester of the participants' senior year is planned to evaluate which aspects of the program had long-lasting effects.

Young adults who are the authors of their own lives have the capacity to make decisions based on internally defined values and goals. Effective career planning requires the ability to reason about complex, often abstract issues. Programs such as Charting Your Journey help students develop a stronger sense of their core identity and use this sense of themselves to reason through complex issues in their lives, including plans for their personal and professional futures.

References

Abes, E. S., & Jones, S. R. (2004). Meaning-making capacity and the dynamics of lesbian college students' multiple dimensions of identity. *Journal of College Student Development, 45*, 612-632.

Abes, E. S., Jones, S. R., & McEwen, M. K. (2007). Reconceptualizing the model of multiple dimensions of identity: The role of meaning-making capacity in the construction of multiple identities. *Journal of College Student Development, 48*, 1-22.

Baxter Magolda, M. B. (2001). *Making their own way: Narratives for transforming higher education to promote self-development.* Sterling, VA: Stylus.

Baxter Magolda, M. B. (2002). Helping students make their way to adulthood: Good company for the journey. *About Campus, 6*(6), 2-9.

Blustein, D. L. (1989). The role of career exploration in the career decision making of college students. *Journal of College Student Development, 30*, 111-117.

Gergen, C., & Vanourek, G. (2008). *Life entrepreneurs: Ordinary people creating extraordinary lives.* San Francisco, CA: Jossey-Bass.

Glaser, B. G., & Strauss, A. L. (1967). *The discovery of grounded theory: Strategies for qualitative research.* Chicago, IL: Aldine Publishing Company.

Jones, S. R., & McEwen, M. K. (2000). A conceptual model of multiple dimensions of identity. *Journal of College Student Development, 41*, 405-414.

Perry, W. G., Jr. (1968). *Forms of intellectual and ethical development in the college years: A scheme.* New York, NY: Holt, Rinehart & Winston.

Pizzolato, J. E. (2005). Creating crossroads for self-authorship: Investigating the provocative moment. *Journal of College Student Development, 46*, 624-641.

Savickas, M. L., Nota, L., Rossier, J., Dauwalder, J. P., Duarte, M. E., Guichard, J., …Van Esbroeck, R. (2009). Life designing: A paradigm for career construction in the 21st century. *Journal of Vocational Behavior, 75*, 239-250.

Swanson, J. L., & Tokar, D. M. (1991). College students' perceptions of barriers to career development. *Journal of Vocational Behavior, 38*, 92-106.

University of Richmond

Destination Unknown: Sophomore Students in Transition

Katybeth Lee and Russell L. Leonard

The Institution

The University of Richmond (UR) is a private, highly selective, four-year university located in Richmond, Virginia. It is largely residential, with 92% of the 2,767 full-time undergraduate students living on campus. Of these students, 59% are women, 23% are U.S. students of color, and 13% do not speak English as a first language. Students hail from 46 states; Washington, DC; Puerto Rico; and 71 countries.

Description of the Initiative

Sophomore students grapple with establishing identity, developing purpose, searching for direction, and making commitments (Lemons & Richman, 1987 in Boivin, Fountain, & Baylis, 2000). This search not only applies to career development but also to personal interests and life goals. Many students experience a "crisis of meaning and purpose" (Boivin et al., p. 5) at this juncture, which may result in a lack of academic goals and commitment to school as well as perceptions that faculty/staff do not care about students (Wilder, 1993 in Boivin et al.). Additionally, sophomores struggle to create connections between academic study and future career goals (Gardner, 2000). Based on the literature related to sophomore struggles and successes, the University of Richmond created Destination Unknown: The Sophomore Experience program in partnership with the University Chaplaincy to address the transition issues of second-year students.

In a study of attrition rates of sophomore men on the University of Richmond campus, Bisese and Fabian (2006) noted that developing more positive and meaningful relationships with faculty outside the classroom, connecting with peers, and addressing stress related to career planning were effective strategies for engaging these students. Graunke and Woosley (2005) also suggested institutions create initiatives to help sophomores discover more about their academic and career interests. To give students the space to undertake this journey and form a worthy dream as well as make the connections with faculty and peers, Daloz Parks (2000) proposed creating mentoring communities, which "provide a place within which young adults may discover themselves becoming more at home...in communities of imagination that distinctly serve young adult meaning making" (p. 157). Destination Unknown took shape around these approaches and is a community seeking to discover how to live a life of consequence through retreat, rigorous reflection, and monthly gatherings. To foster career exploration, the program incorporated several career development strategies, particularly the quest to establish identity, develop purpose, and connect academic and career goals.

Destination Unknown begins with an overnight, off-campus retreat during the first weekend of the fall semester. Letters about the program are mailed to rising sophomores over the summer, and students are accepted on a first-come, first-serve basis. Thus far, all students who have applied for the four offerings have been able to attend, with participation ranging from 10 to 18 students per year (i.e., a total of 60 students from 2006 to 2009). Students are required to pay a $50 deposit with their application, which is returned to them when they arrive at the retreat. There is no cost to participate, and funding is provided by the Office of the Chaplaincy, Student Activities, the Career Development Center, and Student Development. The event is facilitated by faculty, staff, and upper-class students who have previously participated in the program.

The retreat focuses on helping sophomores establish relationships with facilitators and fellow participants in order to create a mentoring community. It is in this context that students can deepen their exploration of their personal interests, values, and academic and career goals. Throughout the weekend, students participate in large-group exercises and meet in family groups consisting of three to four sophomores, a faculty/staff facilitator, and an upper-class peer leader. Following the retreat, the community gathers monthly for dinner and discussion around a variety of topics salient to sophomores at that point in the year.

The exercises and discussion questions are loosely based on the directional points of the compass (i.e., East, West, North, and South) as a metaphor for the direction sophomores are seeking in their quest for purpose and commitment. The East and North sessions are most directly related to career development. Embedded in these sessions are three of the five critical ingredients in career choice interventions Gore and Hunter (2010) discuss: (a) writing, (b) modeling, and (c) building supports.

East: What Are Your New Horizons?

Prior to the retreat, students are asked to complete the Strong Interest Inventory, which is based on Holland's (1973) person-environment typology. At the beginning of this session, students read a series of value-based questions and quickly wrote down their responses in a journal. Next, they paired up and interviewed each other in order to present their partner's salient interests and values to the group and practice articulating an educational and career self-concept (Super, 1992). Following the exercise, a facilitator led a group interpretation of the Strong Interest Inventory, which provides an excellent structure to help students explore how their personal interests connect to potential academic majors and career goals. To conclude the session, students met in family groups to discuss participants' responses to this focused exploration along with possible action steps they plan to take in the coming year.

North: What Is Your Guiding Light?

For this session, a panel of three to five young alumni, faculty, and staff was assembled to share openly about their own career development, including the process they followed to connect their academic majors to their current careers, the crises of meaning and purpose they encountered, and the people who helped them navigate these challenges. Students were encouraged to ask questions. This modeling helps students further differentiate and articulate their own academic and career self-concept (Brown & Ryan Krane, 2000 in Gore & Hunter, 2010). After the panel, students reconvened with their family groups to process their reactions. At the end of this session, they set three to five intentions (e.g., academic, extracurricular, career focused) for the fall semester. They sealed their intentions in an envelope, which was returned to them at the first monthly dinner of the spring semester.

Monthly Dinners

After the retreat, the Destination Unknown community reconvenes monthly for dinner and discussion. These meetings are intended to further nourish the mentoring community, an important support network for students grappling with questions of meaning and purpose (Daloz Parks, 2000), as well as to facilitate transition from career exploration to establishment of career goals and strategies (Super, 1992). Career-related topics of discussion include choosing a study-abroad program to further academic and career goals and pursuing summer opportunities to investigate intended career settings.

Research Design

The evaluation strategy was designed to capture both short- and long-term program impact on participants in terms of what they learned and how they felt about their own academic and career planning. The short-term impact was measured by a survey administered at the end of each retreat consisting of scaled and open-ended questions designed to assess academic and career planning anxiety as well as the formation of a supportive mentoring community.

In addition, participants were either invited to a focus group or e-mailed a survey (i.e., scaled and open-ended questions) in the fall of their junior year to capture how students were applying what they learned and long-term program impacts on their overall sense of well-being. A content analysis was performed on the open-ended and focus group questions to identify consistent themes.

Findings

Initial, End-of-Retreat Results

A high response rate (91.6%) was obtained for the evaluations of the retreat with 55 out of the total 60 participants returning surveys. The results from the scaled items have been consistent across the four years. As the retreats were refined, the evaluations changed slightly. Therefore, Table 1 shows representative results from all of the 18 students who attended the 2009 retreat. Students rated their responses to the survey questions using a 4-point Likert scale (1 = No, 4 = Yes, and 2 and 3 were incremental choices between these two poles).

Table 1

2009 End-of-Retreat Results (N = 18)

	\multicolumn{2}{c}{**No way!**}					\multicolumn{2}{c}{**Yes!**}	
	\multicolumn{2}{c}{1}	\multicolumn{2}{c}{2}	\multicolumn{2}{c}{3}	\multicolumn{2}{c}{4}	Mean
Survey question	*n*	%	*n*	%	*n*	%	*n*	%	
At this point, are you anxious about planning your academics?	0	0	7	39	7	39	4	22	2.82
At this point, are you anxious about planning your career?	2	11	6	33	6	33	4	22	2.61
Have you utilized the campus resources available to you?	3	18	8	47	4	22	2	12	2.1
Did you make connections with students, faculty, and staff?	0	0	0	0	6	33	12	67	3.65
Would you suggest this retreat to students next year?	0	0	0	0	3	17	15	83	3.82

A content analysis of the open-ended question, "What was most meaningful to you in the program?" revealed three consistent themes across the four years. First, participants mentioned the opportunity to meet and get to know new friends through the family group and meal discussions. This suggests the program contributed to the successful establishment of a mentoring community, which is vital for students to delve into the tough questions of identity and purpose (Daloz Parks, 2000) and is foundational to their career development. The second theme was the realization that others shared the same uncertainty regarding majors and career choices. Based on conversations with students, this realization helped them to move past their anxiety and begin more productive career exploration. The third theme was the opportunity to discuss careers with people already in a field, reinforcing the importance of modeling (Gore & Hunter, 2010).

One-Year Results

Of the 60 students who have participated in the four offerings of Destination Unknown, 37 (61.7%) have provided feedback one year later—some in the form of a focus group, and others through online surveys. One-year survey data from two of Destination Unknown communities (i.e., 2008 and 2009, 17 students) comparing student anxiety levels and frequency of using campus resources with initial survey baselines are displayed in Table 2. The findings demonstrate that over the course of the sophomore year, most of the participants reported reduced anxiety regarding academic planning (e.g., choosing a major) and career planning (e.g., stresses of the future), were more aware of the career development resources available to them on campus, and were more inclined to take advantage of support services than before participating in Destination Unknown.

Table 2

2008 and 2009 End-of-Year Results (N = 17)

Survey question	Strongly disagree n	%	Disagree n	%	Uncertain n	%	Agree n	%	Strongly agree n	%	Mean
Destination Unknown helped me to be less anxious about the need to choose a major.	0	0	1	6	3	18	10	59	3	18	3.88
The information I learned regarding my interests and values helped me to choose a major.	0	0	1	6	4	24	11	65	1	6	3.71
The program prompted me to seek additional assistance from the Career Development Center.	0	0	1	6	2	12	7	41	7	41	4.18
As a result of Destination Unknown, I became more knowledgeable about the career resources available to me at the University of Richmond.	0	0	2	12	0	0	7	41	8	47	4.24
Destination Unknown made me more confident that I could handle the stresses and demands of the future.	0	0	1	6	2	12	10	59	4	24	4.00
Participation helped me to be more comfortable relating to faculty and staff.	0	0	0	0	2	12	10	59	5	29	4.18

The following responses to open-ended survey questions suggest some students were able to find a mentoring community where they felt supported and could grapple with establishing identity and developing purpose, two important tasks for sophomore career development:

> I made some good friends. and we still talk about our future plans and have deep conversations about what we want in life. It's so great to be able to talk to other students about goals, worries, and values.

> [Destination Unknown] was an experience that reminded me of how helpful other people can be if you let them.

> I learned that I should take time to be introspective. I should look within myself and listen to where my path is leading me.
>
> I learned that you have to get to know yourself before you think of what career you want to continue in the future.
>
> I learned where my strengths lie and how my major utilizes them.

Many students also commented on maintaining relationships with the faculty and staff facilitators who continued to help guide them as they navigate their academic and career planning.

Further, students reported that they had taken specific actions as a result of their participation in Destination Unknown, such as selecting a course of academic study, creating a major, visiting the Career Development Center for advising, producing and polishing a résumé, seeking out internships, studying abroad, pursuing research, and continuing the process of self-evaluation. These actions demonstrate students' movement from career exploration to establishment of more concrete career goals and strategies.

Conclusion

Going forward, the University hopes to conduct pre- and postassessments of the retreat to more effectively measure its immediate impact. Because career development is an on-going process and students engage in campus life holistically, it is difficult to measure the discrete impact of the Destination Unknown community on student development over time. However, with a foundation of self-evaluation in place, students are better equipped to begin the process of setting goals and taking action.

The strategies Destination Unknown used to address the issues of sophomore transition can easily be adapted by career professionals at a variety of institutions. Offering a mentoring community by gathering groups of sophomores together with faculty, staff, or peer leader facilitators and establishing a safe space to share anxieties and explore dreams helps normalize the college experience and can encourage students to move forward in their academic and career development. Tools, such as the Strong Interest Inventory and focused written exercises, can also help students identify potential academic and career interests. Lastly, older students, young alumni, or established professionals willing to share their own career development stories can model a variety of successful paths for sophomores.

Through Destination Unknown, the importance of helping students connect to a mentoring community in order to support the challenging questions that arise in career exploration and choice was affirmed. Recognizing the value of relationships with faculty, staff, and peers in this process and offering students tools to explore connections between academic and career interests has helped the University more effectively support its sophomores in establishing a solid foundation for their subsequent career development.

References

Bisese, S. D., & Fabian, D. J. (2006). Sophomore men: The forgotten class, the forgotten gender. *Recruitment & Retention in Higher Education, 20*(3), 1-4.

Boivin, M., Fountain, G. A., & Baylis, B. (2000). Meeting the challenges of the sophomore year. In L. A. Schreiner & J. Pattengale (Eds.), *Visible solutions for invisible students: Helping sophomores succeed* (Monograph No. 31, pp. 1-18). Columbia, SC: University of South Carolina, National Resource Center for The First-Year Experience and Students in Transition.

Daloz Parks, S. (2000). *Big questions, worthy dreams: Mentoring young adults in their search for meaning, purpose, and faith*. San Francisco, CA: Jossey-Bass.

Gardner, P. D. (2000). From drift to engagement: Finding purpose and making career connections in the sophomore year. In L. A. Schreiner & J. Pattengale (Eds.), *Visible solutions for invisible students: Helping sophomores succeed* (Monograph No. 31, pp. 67-77). Columbia, SC: University of South Carolina, National Resource Center for The First-Year Experience and Students in Transition.

Gore, P. A., Jr., & Hunter, M. S. (2010). Promoting career success in the second year of college. In M. S. Hunter, B. F. Tobolowsky, J. N. Gardner, S. E. Evenbeck, J. A. Pattengale, M. A. Schaller, L. A. Schreiner, & Associates, *Helping sophomores succeed: Understanding and improving the second-year experience* (pp. 99-113). San Francisco, CA: Jossey-Bass.

Graunke, S. S., & Woosley, S. A. (2005). An exploration of the factors that affect the academic success of college sophomores. *College Student Journal, 39,* 367-377.

Holland, J. L. (1973). *Making vocational choices: A theory of careers*. Englewood Cliffs, NJ: Prentice Hall.

Super, D. E. (1992). Toward a comprehensive theory of career development. In D. Montross & C. Shinkman (Eds.), *Career development: Theory and practice* (pp. 35-64). Springfield, IL: Charles C. Thomas.

Section III:

Career Programs in the Later College Years

University of Utah

A Collaborative Approach to Helping Humanities Students Find Career Success

Liz Leckie, Jessica Mitchell, and Stan Inman

The Institution

The University of Utah, located in Salt Lake City, is a comprehensive research institution, with approximately 22,149 undergraduates enrolled. Of that number, 70% of the undergraduate students are full-time, 85% are from Utah, 75% identify as White, and 55% identify as male.

Description of the Initiative

The University of Utah's College of Humanities is one of the largest undergraduate colleges on campus serving more than 2,500 student majors in 10 departments and programs.[1] During a departmental review, Career Services determined that students in the College of Humanities underused their services compared to other colleges. As a result, Career Services conducted a needs assessment with humanities departmental academic advisors and surveyed peer institutions. From these efforts, the need to assist humanities undergraduates to connect their education with their postcollege career plans became clear.

In spring 2009, Career Services, the College of Humanities, and the University Counseling Center collaborated to create a pilot course entitled Successful Career Planning for Humanities Majors. The upper division, semester-long, one-credit-hour course was designed to educate humanities students about the career decision-making and planning process. Students participated in a series of four one-and-one-half-hour classes and four one-hour individual career-counseling appointments, which instructed them on how to create and implement a personal career plan.

Cognitive Information Processing (CIP) was used as a theoretical framework to design the course (Peterson, Sampson, Lenz, & Reardon, 2002). CIP's focus on engagement in career problem solving and decision making provided a strong foundation upon which to build this career intervention. In addition to CIP, Brown and Ryan Krane's (2000) five features of career counseling, associated with positive changes in career development, were incorporated into the class as follows: (a) written exercises comprised of reflection papers at the end of each class; (b) individualized interpretations and feedback consisting of one-hour, individual appointments with a career counselor, which occurred throughout the semester; (c) world-of-work information gained from students' research into careers of interest; (d) modeling opportunities presented via information interviews with professionals in students' areas of occupational interest; and (e) attention to building support for career choices within one's social network, accomplished through small-group discussions during class. Based on these theories, a number of course objectives were adopted: students will

- Gain an understanding of how to make career decisions
- Develop an understanding of their values, skills, personality traits, interests, life goals, and life roles
- Learn methods and reliable resources for gathering occupational information
- Connect their undergraduate humanities education with possible career competencies and outcomes
- Set personal career goals as they synthesize their self-awareness with information about the world of work
- Develop skills and create materials needed to implement the job search process, including writing résumés, creating professional correspondence, and interviewing that highlights the unique competencies gained through a humanities degree

Seventeen humanities students from a variety of majors enrolled in and completed the course. Of the registered students, 16 of the 17 students were in their junior or senior year. For the majority of these students, graduation was near, and the time available to make a career decision while still an undergraduate was more limited and perhaps more pressing. Further, the fact that academic advisors directly referred these students to take the course and that they registered suggested the students were aware they needed to make a career choice and perhaps were more motivated to do so.

Research Design

Drawing on best practices from university career services offices and professional associations, a range of assessment tools were developed to determine the effectiveness of this pilot course. To measure student learning and growth in terms of the course objectives, a 15-question, Likert-scale assessment was administered at the beginning of the first class and at the end of the final class. The Likert scale consisted of values ranging from 1 (strongly disagree) to 5 (strongly agree). The primary evaluation objective was to examine if students were able improve their understanding and better apply competencies developed through their humanities education to possible career outcomes as a result of learning about and engaging in career planning and decision making.

In addition to the pre- and postassessments, quantitative and qualitative data were gathered through the final course evaluation that included 25 Likert-scale questions as well as three open-ended questions. This assessment instrument solicited feedback on pedagogical methods, specific assignments, presenters, and course expectations.

Additional qualitative data were gathered from student writing assignments and the interview processes. At the end of each class, students identified the most significant elements of that specific session and listed one action item that they could implement in their career planning. In the final class, students met with a group of employers representing a range of profit, nonprofit, and higher education organizations that offered interesting opportunities for which humanities majors would qualify. Prior to this session, students researched the companies and organizations and then introduce themselves to the employers as if they were applying for a job. In particular, students were asked to articulate the unique skills and competencies gained through their humanities majors and discuss how these would benefit the company. The employers assessed the quality of the students' interviews and provided written individual feedback and general oral feedback to the entire class.

This final evaluation provided an opportunity to receive information related to students' learning and application through the eyes of prospective employers.

Findings

The results from the pre- and postassessments were analyzed to determine whether the course led to changes for these humanities students in terms of their career planning readiness and ability. Initial findings indicated that there was improvement in all areas. Given the small sample size and the fact that this was a pilot program, these are preliminary findings and warrant further study.

Findings were divided into three primary areas: (a) general awareness of the career decision-making process (Table 1), (b) knowledge of the relationships among academic majors and self-awareness to possible career choices (Table 2), and (c) the ability to set personal career goals and implement a career search using effective career planning tools relevant to a humanities degree (Table 3).

As indicated in Table 1, when asked about their general awareness of the career decision-making process, humanities students indicated neutrality at the pre-assessment and higher levels of agreement in terms of familiarity with the career decision-making process at the postassessment. Humanities students also moved from neutrality to agreement in terms of their awareness of their own decision-making style and in their awareness of the tools needed to make an effective career decision. These findings indicate that by the conclusion of the course students had gained greater awareness of various aspects of the career decision-making process.

Table 1

Students Awareness of the Decision-Making Process

Item	Pretest mean	Posttest mean	Difference
I understand the career decision-making process.	2.78	4.12	1.34
I am aware of my decision-making style.	2.89	4.12	1.23
I have the tools to make effective and complex decisions about careers.	2.67	4.24	1.57

In Table 2, humanities students also indicated neutrality in the pre-assessment regarding their knowledge of the relationship between academic majors and possible careers. By the post-assessment, students moved to agreement in terms of their understanding about this relationship. Likewise, students also indicated an increased awareness of the career-related skills they developed through their undergraduate humanities degree. These findings indicate an increase in students' understanding of and ability to articulate the relationships between an undergraduate major and future career opportunities.

Table 2

Students Awareness of the Relationship Between Majors and Career Options

Item	Pretest mean	Posttest mean	Difference
I can describe how my major relates to my future career options.	3.39	4.24	0.85
I am aware of the career-related skills that I have developed through my education.	3.22	4.24	1.02

Table 3 shows that this cohort of humanities students initially indicated neutrality in terms of their ability to set personal career goals and to implement a career search using effective career planning tools. By the end of the course, these students were better able to make a short list of careers of interest and set realistic career goals. Students in this class experienced positive movement in terms of the tangibles of the job search process and the implementation of their goals, such as articulating the unique skills and competencies gained as a part of their humanities degree, interviewing, and résumé writing.

Table 3

Students' Ability to Set Personal Career Goals

Item	Pretest mean	Posttest mean	Difference
I am able to make a short list of my careers of interest.	3.39	4.41	1.02
I am able to communicate/market my skills to an employer.	3.28	4.35	1.07
I have set realistic short-term goals that I can accomplish this semester related to my career.	3.00	3.88	0.88
I know how to interview for a job or internship.	3.33	4.12	0.79
I can write a quality, targeted résumé and cover letter.	3.28	4.24	0.96
I am confident that my major choice will lead to careers of interest.	3.83	4.24	0.41
I am confident in my ability to make complex decisions about my career.	3.41	4.12	0.71
I am aware of my interests and values and the role these play in my career decision.	3.72	4.41	0.69

In addition, the findings in Table 3 also reveal divergence between students' confidence in academic choices as related to career outcomes and knowledge of available career resources. There was a series of questions related to students' confidence in their career decision-making ability, their self-awareness, and the links to their academic choices. Students were generally confident in their ability to make complex decisions about careers at the beginning of the course, and there was little change by the end of the course. Students also expressed confidence about the relationship between their undergraduate humanities majors and future career outcomes, and again, there was little increase at the end of the course concerning this confidence. Also related to confidence, students generally understood the role self-knowledge and self-discovery play in the career decision-making process, and findings indicated little movement at the end of course.

In contrast to these previously articulated findings, students initially expressed disagreement in their awareness and use of career planning resources (see Table 3). At the conclusion of the course, however, students had greater awareness of these resources and indicated they were more likely to use them. This change represents the largest impact of the career-planning course.

Conclusion

The data from this limited study indicate that the career class helped humanities students increase their awareness of the career decision-making process, understanding of how this process connected their academic areas of study to possible career choices, and use of career planning tools. There was a notable divergence between the students' agreement about their confidence in their academic choices, decision-making ability, and self-awareness, and their awareness and use of career-planning resources. However, these findings indicate that at the conclusion of this course, students demonstrated the strongest movement in their awareness of the career decision-making process and campus resources available to assist and support them through this process.

For many reasons, it is important for students to get the most out of college and learn a broad range of skills and capacities so they can deal with changes in the world. The humanities provide opportunities for students to learn about the histories, stories, languages, philosophies, tensions, and conflicts that make up contemporary society. Despite the important skills and knowledge that humanities students gain through their studies, sometimes they have difficulty translating these into possible career options and may not be aware that many occupations could require additional study, training, or on-the-job experiences, which may involve considerable time and financial sacrifice beyond their baccalaureate degree.

Without explicit and intentional conversations with humanities students about how to prepare for their career after their degree, students often express uncertainty and lack of confidence and can feel overwhelmed. Consequently, the need to provide extensive career advising that includes assessment of personal interests, aptitudes, and skills; directed career exploration connected to their studies; and planning and networking opportunities is critical.

Although there is still much to be learned about how students in humanities and liberal arts areas understand the career decision-making process connected to their chosen course of study, this pilot study leads to interesting implications and questions for career and academic advisors. Career planning and decision-making programs explicitly connected to students programs of study, such as the one outlined here, can provide more nuanced and directed understandings of students processes than general or generic career planning programs. Grouping students by their decided courses of study provides career counselors an opportunity to understand more clearly the perceived and actual barriers that humanities students, and perhaps students in other areas of study, face as they create their postbaccalaureate plans.

For career service practitioners this pilot course and its findings illuminate that at the core of our work lies the need for collaboration. Through collaboration between career services and academic departments, career services practitioners, who often serve as the link between employers and the university, can develop an increased awareness and appreciation of academic majors thereby facilitating outreach to employers. In addition, the shared responsibilities between academic departments and careers services can only serve to enhance student learning about career decision making as related to major.

Still, further research is needed in order to understand more fully the neutrality humanities students experience when they engage in the career planning process. In particular, longitudinal studies of similar classes may provide greater depth and nuance of the initial findings provided herein. Additional studies that focus on the neutrality that humanities and liberal arts students experience in relation to the career planning process and the confidence that they express in their academic areas of study can provide insights that may create more effective and collaborative college career services. Our understanding of student neutrality may be furthered by using student interviews and focus groups designed in ways that highlight and bring a qualitative lens to this concept. More specific questions concentrating on humanities student neutrality may tease out the meanings of students' uncertainty or lack of clarity about the connections between their studies and careers and may provide the needed answers to strengthen career counseling and related programming. This project illuminates a beginning to this conversation in which others are encouraged to join.

Notes

[1]The major departments and programs in the College of Humanities at the University of Utah include Asian Studies, Communication, English, History, International Studies, Languages and Literature, Latin American Studies, Linguistics, Middle East Studies, Philosophy, and University Writing Program.

References

Brown, S. D., & Ryan Krane, N. E. (2000). Four (or five) sessions and a cloud of dust: Old assumptions and new observations about career counseling. In S. D. Brown & R. W. Lent (Eds.), *Handbook of counseling psychology* (pp. 740-766). New York, NY: John Wiley & Sons.

Peterson, G. W., Sampson, J. P., Lenz, J. G., & Reardon, R. C. (2002). A cognitive information processing approach to career problem solving and decision making. In D. Brown (Ed.), *Career choice and development* (4th ed., pp. 312-369). San Francisco, CA: Jossey-Bass.

THE OHIO STATE UNIVERSITY

INTERDISCIPLINARY CAREER PREPARATION: PROFESSIONAL PATHWAYS SEMINARS

Jessica Mercerhill and Britney Kyle

The Institution

The Ohio State University (OSU), located in Columbus, is a world-class research university and the leading comprehensive teaching and research institution in the state. This four-year, residential institution is currently the largest public university, enrolling approximately 40,000 full-time undergraduate students per year. The student population is comprised of approximately 48% women and 14% minority students.

Description of the Initiative

In 2006, the College of Arts and Sciences at OSU realized liberal arts students required more guidance in terms of concrete career paths that could be pursued after graduation. To that end, the Professional Pathways program was created to introduce students to a variety of interdisciplinary careers that do not conform to the curriculum of a single academic department.

The program consists of separate seminars for career exploration in urban education, entrepreneurship, health care, nonprofit organizations, social justice, public affairs, Wall Street, higher education and student affairs, and civic engagement. Course goals include (a) introducing students to current professional issues in the field; (b) offering students the opportunity to explore professional career paths; (c) providing an overview of professional opportunities to all students, including nonmajors; and (d) helping students understand the relationship between professional pathway preparation and degree planning. The initiative was given an additional administrative mandate to achieve financial autonomy within three years.

The Professional Pathways program is a unique opportunity for students to select and investigate a profession they are interested in as a free elective while still in college. Offered in 19 sections, as of 2009, a total of 378 students have participated in the one- or two-credit-hour seminars. Sections are capped at 18 students to encourage more interactive learning in a small classroom environment.

Housed within the Arts and Sciences' Office of Interdisciplinary Programs, rather than in a specific academic unit, Professional Pathways program administrators are able to facilitate relationships and course development across the entire OSU campus. Seminars are designed to be interdisciplinary and attract students from a variety of colleges and disciplines (Table 1; Figure 1). Although the majority of those enrolled are from the Arts and Sciences, it has become apparent that even students in professional disciplines benefit from this career information as evidenced by the continually rising enrollments from the professional colleges.

Table 1

Professional Pathways Enrollment Divided by College

College	2006-2007 (*n* = 112) n	%	2007-2009 (*n* = 100) n	%	2008-2009 (*n* = 167) n	%	Combined (*N* = 378) N	%
Allied Medical Professions	4	3.6	1	1	0	0	5	1.3
Arts & Sciences	93	83.1	70	70	118	70.5	281	74.3
Business	0	0	2	2.0	17	10.2	19	5.0
Continuing Education	0	0	1	1.0	2	1.2	3	0.1
Education & Human Ecology	4	3.6	4	4.0	1	0.6	9	2.4
Engineering	0	0	3	3.0	4	2.4	7	1.9
Exploration/Undecided	1	0.9	4	4.0	7	4.2	11	2.9
Food, Agricultural, & Environmental Sciences	1	0.9	0	0	1	0.6	2	0.1
Graduate School (all majors)	0	0	1	1.0	0	0	1	0
Music	0	0	0	0	3	1.8	3	0.1
Nursing	1	0.9	10	10.0	5	2.9	16	4.2
Pharmacy	5	4.5	3	3.0	8	4.8	16	4.2
Social Work	3	2.7	1	1.0	1	0.6	5	1.3

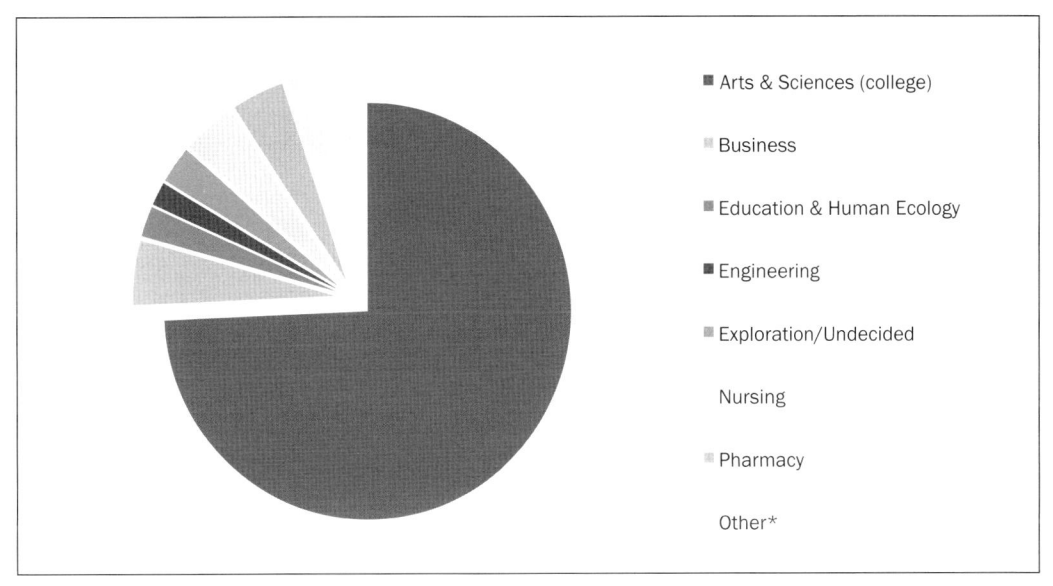

Figure 1. Depiction of student enrollment by college.
*Other programs include Allied Medical Professions; Continuing Ed; Environmental & Natural Resources; Food, Agricultural, & Environmental Sciences; Graduate School (all majors); Music; and Social Work.

While Professional Pathways seminars are open to all OSU students, they are geared toward sophomores and juniors. By targeting students in the middle of their academic career, these seminars can provide information on steps that students should take to prepare for future careers before graduate school and employment applications are due.

The seminars use a variety of methods to provide exposure to different career opportunities, including tailoring course content to the specific interests of the students and bringing in professional guest speakers. These guest speakers not only provide an overview of their experience in and understanding of the field, they explain the path they followed to enter their occupation. Students are then given the opportunity to ask questions and interact with these professionals. All courses contain reading and writing assignments to provide a foundation in relevant literature as well as opportunities for students to analyze and reflect on the career. To ensure relevancy and authenticity, seminars are taught by instructors who have worked in the field representing the course topic. As such, instructors are not limited to University faculty but may include professional members of the community.

The four stages of Gottfredson's Theory of Circumscription and Compromise in Career Guidance and Counseling (Gottfredson, 2004) are incorporated into the program: (a) cognitive growth, (b) self creation, (c) circumscription (the elimination of less appealing options), and (d) compromise (the acknowledgment of external constraints). This construct assists students in matching their own skill sets with careers that may be accessible to them and eliminating choices that may not be a good fit.

Research Design

To evaluate the success and capture a holistic picture of the Professional Pathways program, direct and indirect assessments have focused on (a) the realization of the initial four program goals and (b) the continued program growth and development. Data relating to the realization of program goals largely come from student feedback, including self-reported career plans and placement, which are completed at several stages in the program. Students take pre- and posttests during the class measuring their level of understanding and preparation for a profession. They also complete a course evaluation form during the last week of class. One year following the course, an e-mail survey is administered to students asking them to discuss their career plans in the context of their seminar. Additionally, demographic data and enrollment trends are gathered each spring on student population variables, including gender, honors or scholars affiliation, ethnicity, class rank, and enrollment college. Descriptive statistics are recorded to identify programmatic growth as well as proportions and percentages of students from each demographic group.

Program growth and development is measured by course offerings and student enrollment, as well as the program's ability to incorporate student and instructor feedback into future course offerings. To this end, yearly reports are submitted to the OSU Committee on Curriculum and Instruction by the Office of Interdisciplinary Programs detailing the program's capacity to adjust instructional methods to improve the seminars' ability to meet program goals. Moreover, instructors are given summary sheets with student comments so that they can incorporate this feedback into future classes.

Findings

While seminars are geared toward second- and third-year students, seniors are the largest demographic (Figure 2). The data do not provide an explanation for this occurrence; however, it may be a result of students looking for more elective coursework in their final year or a result of students hoping to change career paths late in their undergraduate program. Similar numbers of males and females enroll in Professional Pathways courses, and 40% of Pathways students are either honors or scholars students (25% honors; 15% scholars). Additionally, the program has grown in terms of number of seminars offered as well as raw enrollment numbers.

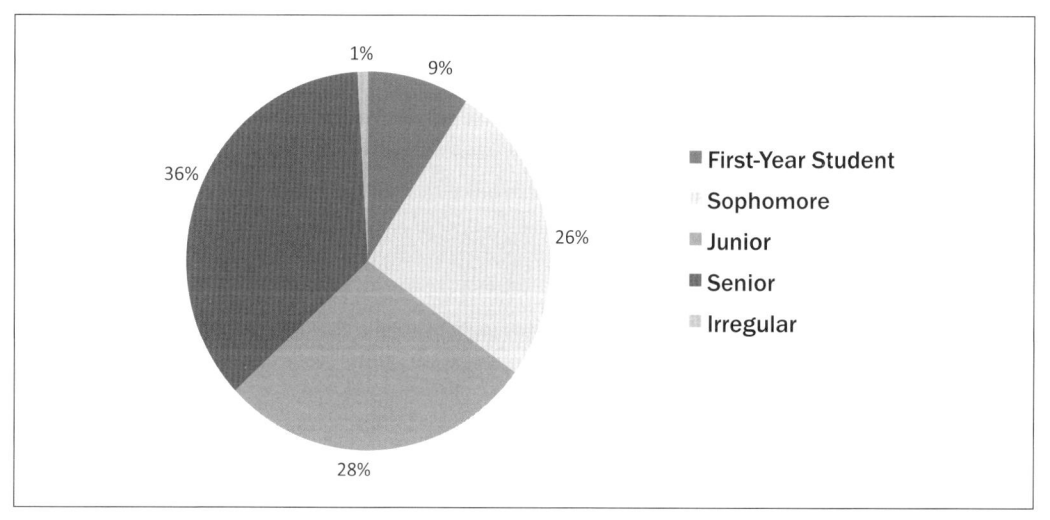

Figure 2. Professional Pathways student enrollment by class standing.

Attainment of program goals was primarily assessed through student feedback at several stages of the program. Comparison of a pre- and postcourse assessment (105 students completed the test for a 28% response rate) revealed that only 40% of students felt they knew how to prepare for a career in their field at the start of the course; whereas, 97% felt able to prepare for this career upon completion of the class. Some variation existed between seminars: students in the health-care seminar were more aware of how to prepare for their chosen career at the beginning of the course than those in other seminars. Similarly, 24% of students precourse were aware of the roles and duties within the field versus 97% postcourse. Once again, students in health-care seminars were more aware of the roles and duties at the start of the course (31%). Further, while 59% of students precourse stated that they understood how the field affects other disciplines and society as a whole, 98% reported that they understood this interdisciplinarity at course completion.

In addition to the pre- and postcourse test, students were asked to complete an evaluation at the end of each quarter. Data were gathered from 175 students, representing a 46% response rate (Table 2). These evaluations demonstrated that 91% of students felt that Professional Pathways seminars helped them clarify their career goals, and 96% would recommend the class to another student.

Table 2

Student Evaluations of Professional Pathways Seminars (n = 175)

Student Evaluation Questions	Average	% Agree
I made the effort to know the professor well enough to ask for a letter of recommendation for an internship or study abroad application.	3.41	48
Participation in the seminar made me think about taking more courses in this area.	4.21	83
Participation in the seminar helped clarify my career goals or made me aware of new careers.	4.36	91
The workload was not too much for a one/two credit-hour course.	4.15	81
It was clear what was expected of me in the seminar.	4.48	93
The professor was knowledgeable about the subject matter.	4.74	97
I would recommend this seminar to other students.	4.67	96

Note. Average of response on a 5-point scale, where 1 = strongly disagree to 5 = strongly agree. % agree figure is the percentage of those who answered either *agree* or *strongly agree*.

An e-mail survey asking students to reflect on their experiences was sent one year after completing the seminar. Of the 212 students contacted, 27 students (12.7%) responded. All indicated that the seminar was useful in preparing them for their potential career. Additionally, the majority of the respondents (25 students) still planned to pursue a career relating to their seminar. Of these, 10 were currently applying to a graduate or professional program in their discipline, and five were either employed or enrolled in a graduate/professional program in the field. In contrast, exit surveys gathered from 1,288 graduating students in all Arts and Sciences majors showed that only 34% of students planned to seek employment in their area of study. These data suggest that while disciplinary majors may not prepare students for future careers, interdisciplinary Professional Pathways seminars do.

The financial autonomy of the Professional Pathways program is evaluated on a yearly basis and is accomplished when the revenue generated through student enrollment is sufficient to cover the costs of instructional and administrative support. As the program has grown, it has become self-supporting fiscally.

Conclusion

Most OSU Arts and Sciences students report in the exit survey that they do not plan to pursue a career in the field in which they majored. While this may seem counterintuitive to those who would argue a university education is primarily designed to prepare students for the professional world, OSU believes there is also great value in pursuing a liberal arts education. The Professional Pathways program bridges these two seemingly divergent higher education goals by allowing students to explore potential careers while still experiencing the diverse learning curriculum of a liberal arts major program. The seminars prepare students for real-world jobs by providing knowledge of those jobs and helping students clarify their career goals and begin to plan for a profession earlier in their educational experience.

Professional Pathways will continue with its current assessment and delivery methods in the foreseeable future. To better reach the targeted population of second- and third-year students, program administrators are working with academic advisors to ensure that these students are receiving information about the courses. Future alterations to the program will be guided by patterns that emerge from the data suggesting adjustments that need to be made. For institutions wishing to create a similar initiative, program components that seem to be especially effective are (a) a staffing model using instructors who have worked in the field and offer real world experience, (b) guest speaker presentations from professionals in the community giving students insight from multiple perspectives, (c) flexible scheduling and course content to tailor the seminar to students' specific needs and interests, and (d) small class sizes to encourage interactive learning.

The Professional Pathways program has proven successful in both career preparation and exposure to employment opportunities that are unassociated with traditional academic majors and will continue to be an integral part of The Ohio State University's student career development focus.

References

Gottfredson L. S. (2004). Applying Gottfredson's theory of circumscription and compromise in career guidance and counseling. In S. D. Brown & R. W. Lent (Eds.), *Career development and counseling: Putting theory and research to work* (pp. 71- 100). Hoboken, NJ: John Wiley & Sons.

The Ohio State University

Qualified Undergraduate Interview Candidate: Transitioning to Professional Interviews

Sarah Steenrod, Kristin Schrader, Pam Park-Curry, and Margie Bogenschutz

The Institution

The Ohio State University is a four-year, world-class, public research university and the leading comprehensive teaching and research institution in the state. Ohio State is a multicampus university with a main residential campus in Columbus and four regional campuses. The enrollment of undergraduate students on the Columbus campus is approximately 41,300 and the population demographics are 48% women, 14% minorities, and 7% international students.

Description of the Initiative

During the summer of 2003 and with the influence of the best seller *Good to Great* by Jim Collins (2001), the staff of the Fisher College of Business Office of Career Management (OCM) at The Ohio State University developed an office-wide mission: To be every employer's favorite place to recruit and to have the best prepared job seekers. Focusing on this mission allowed OCM to address job recruiter feedback that students often had unprofessional résumés and were unprepared for interviews. Additionally, recruiters noted that if they found high-quality candidates at the Fisher College of Business, they would return often to recruit. Based on this feedback, the Qualified Undergraduate Interview Candidate (QUIC) program was created in 2003 to assist students in transitioning to professional interviews.

The development of the QUIC program was informed by Holland's (1973) theory of person-environment fit. According to Holland, an individual is often attracted to and performs well in an environment that is congruent with his or her personality. The QUIC program encourages students to reflect on their personality, skills, and values in relation to company culture and job descriptions. A student with a social, outgoing personality might choose to interview for a marketing or sales internship, while an investigative, detail-oriented student with excellent analytical abilities might choose to interview for a finance or accounting internship. In order to interview successfully, students must understand themselves and be able to communicate to an employer why they are a good fit for the position and company and how they will add value.

The QUIC program is a six-step process, which includes participation in and passing a mock interview. Upon completion of the program students become qualified interview candidates and gain access to FisherConnect, an online employment data management system. This allows students the opportunity to interview with recruiters through the College of Business. The six steps are

1. Admission into a major within the Fisher College of Business
2. Development of a professional résumé

3. Creation of a profile and uploading a résumé to the FisherConnect data management system
4. Completion of five online QUIC modules: (a) introduction to QUIC, (b) OCM policies, (c) tutorial on using FisherConnect for interviewing, (d) professionalism in the job search, and (e) effective interviewing strategies in preparation for QUIC interview. Progression through the modules is dependent on passing summary quizzes with a perfect score.
5. Scheduling and passing of a 60-minute QUIC mock interview
6. Using FisherConnect to search for jobs or internships

Staff conduct all QUIC interviews to provide content and evaluation consistency. A pool of 10 staff and graduate administrative assistants conduct the QUIC interviews, offering numerous interview scheduling opportunities. Each interview is put in the context of an actual company and position, so students must research both the organization and the job for which they are interviewing, simulating an actual interview experience. The companies used for QUIC interviews are selected from those who recruit on campus. The job descriptions are drafted from actual positions previously posted in FisherConnect.

All interviewers use the same list of questions and a rubric to guide their scoring (see Appendix A). New graduate administrative assistants and staff participate in training sessions at the beginning of the academic year to review the QUIC interview process, which includes logistical aspects and instruction on how to evaluate a student's responses and provide feedback. Graduate administrative assistants also have the opportunity to shadow several QUIC interviews with staff members prior to conducting interviews on their own. Ongoing discussions occur at staff meetings throughout the academic year to address questions or specific scenarios that arise.

A passing score on the QUIC interview is 86 or above on a 100-point scale. Students scoring 80-85 are required to successfully complete an additional 20-minute practice session before becoming QUIC certified. The interviewer determines which questions required a stronger response, and the student returns for a follow-up appointment to respond to those questions (see Appendix B). The additional practice session ensures that a student applies the constructive feedback given in the QUIC interview to future interviews. Scores 79 or below are nonpassing, and students are required to repeat the entire QUIC interview. After passing the QUIC interview, students are given access to FisherConnect to search for a job or internship.

Research Design

To evaluate the program, the OCM collects quantitative and qualitative data from both recruiters and students. Employers are also asked to assess students' professionalism and interview skills. Prior to QUIC's implementation in 2003, data were gathered from employers using a paper survey format; however, the employer response rate for the 2002-2003 academic year was only 20% (i.e., 63 surveys returned out of a possible 312), and an online format has been used in subsequent assessments resulting in a higher return rate.

To gather student input, in 2008-2009, all 1,036 QUIC interview participants were e-mailed an electronic survey following their QUIC interview, and 123 students (11.9%) responded. The survey asked for anonymous feedback (to encourage more open and honest responses) on the students' experience with the program and whether QUIC met their expectations (see Appendix C). Responses were measured using a 3-point scale, and averages and standard deviations on each question were calculated.

In addition to the e-mailed student survey, QUIC participants completed a pre- and posttest survey during fall quarter 2008 to assess the impact of the mock interview on their confidence levels (see Appendix D). Upon checking in for a QUIC interview, students were given a pretest paper survey asking them to rate their confidence in their (a) ability to provide specific examples to behavior-based questions, (b) aptitude for offering evidence of fit with the company, (c) skill in closing the interview, and (d) overall self-assurance going into an interview. The same survey was administered immediately upon completion of their QUIC interview. Data were analyzed using matched pairs *t*-tests comparing confidence levels before and after the QUIC interview. Quantitative data were also collected on the pass-fail rates on the QUIC interviews as well as average scores assessed by each interviewer.

All data are discussed by QUIC interviewers on a quarterly basis to determine whether modifications are necessary to the content of the constructive feedback given to students.

Findings

Tables 1, 2, and 3 reflect data from pre- and post-QUIC employer surveys. Table 1 illustrates employer feedback from 2002-2003, the year immediately prior to the implementation of the QUIC program and shows recruiters' opinions to be less favorable of students' ability to share knowledge about the company and use good examples to support their answers compared to the 2008-2009 academic year. Students' ability to convince the recruiter they should be hired was slightly lower in the most recent school year compared to preprogram data, a finding that could be the result of students' lack of confidence due to the current economic recession.

Table 1

Comparison of Recruiter Evaluations Before and After Program Implementation

	2002-2003 Before program implementation		2008-2009 After program implementation	
	n	*M*	*n*	*M*
Could share knowledge about company	63	3.71	141	4.03
Convinced recruiter they should be hired	63	3.76	141	3.70
Used good examples to support their answers	62	3.56	141	4.06

Note. Mean of response on a 5-point scale, where 1 = disagree, 3 = neutral, 5 = agree.

Overall, the QUIC program employer evaluations indicated that Fisher candidates performed very favorably. Tables 2 and 3 identify recruiters' perception of Fisher students and are measured on a 5-point scale (1 = disagree, 3 = neutral, 5 = agree). More than 80% of the employers agreed or somewhat agreed that students had appropriate skills in all areas except (a) having a strong introduction (70%), (b) convincing the recruiter they should be hired (65%), (c) providing enough details in their examples (74%), and (d) asking how they could follow up (79%). Yet, even in these lowest ranked categories, the majority of the recruiters felt that students demonstrated the skill.

Table 2

2008-2009 Recruiter Evaluation of Interview Introduction (n = 143)

	M	*SD*	Percentage responding agree or somewhat agree
Were professionally dressed	4.90	.38	99
Were on time to the interview	4.88	.45	99
Greeted recruiter in a positive manner	4.96	.23	100

Note. Mean of response on a 5-point scale, where 1 = disagree, 3 = neutral, 5 = agree.

Table 3

2008-2009 Recruiter Evaluation of Interviewee (n = 141)

	M	*SD*	Percentage responding agree or somewhat agree
Used clear examples to answer behavioral questions	4.13	.74	87
Could share knowledge about company	4.03	.91	81
Asked thoughtful questions about the position and company	4.33	.82	89
Demonstrated fit with the company	4.11	.77	85
Had a strong introduction	3.86	.82	70
Provided examples that they have skills needed for the position	4.29	.76	88
Convinced recruiter they should be hired	3.70	.98	65
Used good examples to support their answers	4.06	.83	82
Provided enough details in their examples	3.99	.84	74
Asked thoughtful questions	4.28	.81	88
Expressed clear interest in the company and the position	4.45	.76	89
Asked how they could follow up	4.17	1.01	79

Note. Mean of response on a 5-point scale, where 1 = disagree, 3 = neutral, 5 = agree.

Qualitative feedback from employers also highlights the success of the QUIC program as demonstrated by this recruiter's remark:

> I am an undergrad alum and have recruited twice previously. Those visits were disappointing in terms of the quality of candidates and quantity. I considered passing this year, notwithstanding the great rating of the business school. Glad I didn't—the quality of the 12 candidates was superb.

In addition, students' perceptions of the QUIC program are favorable. According to one student, the QUIC interview has contributed real-world interview success:

> I was fortunate enough to pass on my first try, but I know that I grew into a far better interviewee because of my QUIC interview. In fact, I have received a job offer from every interview I have had since!

Tables 4 and 5 highlight students' perceptions of the program's introductory modules and the feedback provided by their QUIC interviewer. The 3-point scale (1 = below expectations, 2 = met expectations, 3 = exceeded expectations) used for this evaluation showed that student satisfaction with the QUIC program modules was favorable in preparing for the QUIC process and the QUIC interview itself. Almost all of the students (99%) believed the QUIC program met or exceeded their expectations in preparing them for the on-campus interview process.

Table 4

2008-2009 Student Evaluation of QUIC Interview Modules (n = 122)

	M	*SD*	Percentage reporting program met or exceeded expectations
QUIC interview process	2.38	.50	99
Preparation for QUIC interview	2.35	.53	98
On-campus interview process	2.30	.48	99

Note. Mean of response on a 3-point scale, where 1 = below expectations, 2 = met expectations, 3 = exceeded expectations.

Table 5

2008-2009 Student Evaluation of QUIC Interviewer (n = 122)

	M	SD	Percentage reporting program met or exceeded expectations
Approachability	2.69	.47	100
Clarity of communication	2.78	.42	100
Knowledge of interviewing	2.78	.44	99
Delivery of constructive feedback	2.88	.32	100

Note. Mean of response on a 3-point scale, where 1 = below expectations, 2 = met expectations, 3 = exceeded expectations.

The confidence survey conducted in fall 2008 also supports the effectiveness of the QUIC program demonstrating an increase in student confidence over all four variables assessed (Table 6). This survey was administered to the 479 students who participated in the QUIC program for that academic year, and 250 students (52%) responded. Students' overall confidence going into an interview increased, on average, from 2.88 to 3.32 (i.e., on a 4-point scale, 4 = very confident) after going through the QUIC interview. All of these comparisons were significant ($p < .001$).

Table 6

Fall 2008 Pre- and Post-QUIC Interview Student Confidence (n = 250)

	Preprogram M	Preprogram SD	Postprogram M	Postprogram SD	t
Ability to be specific when answering questions	2.94	.64	3.26	.72	-7.07***
Ability to demonstrate fit with the company	3.02	.64	3.35	.69	-7.25***
Ability to close the interview	2.85	.69	3.24	.78	-7.15***
Overall confidence	2.88	.58	3.32	.62	-10.49***

Note. Mean of response on a 4-point scale, where 1 = not at all confident and 4 = very confident.
*$p < .05$. **$p < .01$. ***$p < .001$.

Conclusion

The QUIC program is having a positive impact on students and their confidence; therefore, a continued goal will be to encourage more students, including those who do not necessarily want to interview on campus, to take advantage of the opportunities to practice and develop their interviewing skills by completing the QUIC program. The QUIC program has become an embedded part of the Fisher culture with increasing numbers of students completing QUIC interviews each year. During the 2003-2004 academic year, 600 students completed a QUIC interview with this number increasing 72.6% to 1,036 students during the 2008-2009 academic year.

The increased use of the QUIC program is due in part to partnerships the OCM has developed with Fisher courses to help inform students about the QUIC program. The instructors of a required business skills course within Fisher, which is taken by more than 1,000 students each year, have created an assignment that requires the students to complete the QUIC modules. By completing the QUIC modules, all students are introduced to the QUIC program and become eligible to schedule a QUIC interview. In addition to the QUIC modules assignment, one class session is devoted to career management, and the OCM gives a 90-minute presentation covering the QUIC program, résumé writing, and interviewing. The office also offers a job search preparation course, and all students in the course are required to become QUIC certified as a class assignment. In 2008-2009, 187 students took this class.

By combining online self-learning modules with an intensive, one-on-one, hour-long interview and using graduate assistant resources, QUIC has proven to be an effective and efficient career development model that could successfully be duplicated on other campuses. Within the one-hour interview appointment, a staff member can not only conduct a mock interview and provide a student with extensive feedback regarding the interview but may also be able to spend time critiquing a student's résumé and answering a few questions related to the student's career goals. The skills students learn in the QUIC program empower them to confidently transition to being a professional interview candidate ready to impress recruiters and enter the world of work.

References

Collins, J. (2001). *Good to great*. New York, NY: HarperCollins.

Holland, J. L. (1973). *Making vocational choices: A theory of careers*. Englewood Cliffs, NJ: Prentice Hall.

Appendix A

Fisher College of Business
Office of Career Management
QUIC Interview Assessment
Preparing undergraduates for an effective job/internship search

Student Name: _____ **Dot#:** _____ **Grad Date:** _____

Evaluator/Company: _____ **QI Date:** _____

Job Description: _____ **First QUIC Interview?** _____

Interview Standard	Total Points	Student's Points
Professional Presentation:		
Student arrives and is prepared to begin on time	5	_____
Student is dressed professionally	5	_____
Student brings a polished copy of his/her résumé	5	_____
Student has a firm hand shake	3	_____
Student maintains eye contact	3	_____
Sitting posture is straight and attentive	3	_____
Student speaks clearly and understandably	3	_____
Student shows a positive attitude and enthusiasm	3	_____

Effective Interviewing Skills:

Q1. Tell me about yourself.
Summary – why Fisher and why here today
Highlights strengths
Highlights unique experiences
Makes connection to job

1   2   3   4   5   6   7   8   9   10   _____

Q2. Why did you choose your major?
Evidence of what they LIKE about major (displays excitement)
Provides reasons major is a good fit
Researched other majors

1   2   3   4   5   6   7   8   9   10   _____

Q3. What interests you about our company?
Shows knowledge of what they are looking for in organization and how company fits criteria
Evidence of research on company – cites details that are not obvious
Displays interest and fit with company culture/values

1   2   3   4   5   6   7   8   9   10   _____

Q4. Behavioral Based Questions

	Q1	Q2	Q3
Situation			
Task			
Action			
Result			

2   4   6   8   10   12   14   16   18   20   _____

Q5. Why should I hire you?
Characteristics important to company regarding job description
Sets themselves apart from competition in meaningful way
Gives a trait and cites specific evidence - mini behavioral based

1   2   3   4   5   6   7   8   9   10   _____

Q6. What questions do you have for me?
Student should have at least three questions to ask
Questions are specific to company and diverse in type

1   2   3   4   5   _____

Q7. Is there anything else you think I should know about you?
Highlights any experiences relevant but not previously mentioned
Displays enthusiasm in working for the company
Gives some sort of answer

1   2   3   4   5   _____

TOTAL POINTS   100   _____

_____Pass: 86 or Higher

_____Nonpass: 1-79

    Made QUIC by _____

             On _____

Reservations: 80-85
- ☐ Introduction
- ☐ Company knowledge/connection with job
- ☐ Behavioral questions
- ☐ Why should I hire you?
- ☐ Closure

Appendix B

Fisher College of Business
Office of Career Management
QUIC Interview More Practice Needed —STUDENT COPY

QUIC Interview Company: _____

Date of first QUIC Interview: _____

Students who score 80 to 85 points on a 100-point scale are required to pass an additional 20-minute practice session before becoming QUIC certified.

Below are the steps you now need to take to complete the QUIC process:

1. Sign up for a QUIC Interview **More Practice Needed** appointment with the person doing your QUIC interview or at the front desk.

    The appointment is scheduled for (date):_____

    With (person):_____

2. Research the same company that you did for your previous QUIC interview.

3. Review the check boxes below to see where you need the most practice.

4. Practice on your own before attending the practice session.

5. Attend the 20-minute practice session at your allotted time. *
    *The practice session will be less formal than your first QUIC interview, and you do not need to dress up to attend.

Refer to the check boxes below for the areas on which you should focus most in your practice.

- ☐ Introduction
- ☐ Company knowledge/connection with job
- ☐ Behavioral questions
- ☐ Why should I hire you
- ☐ Closure

Appendix C

Fisher College of Business
Office of Career Management
QUIC Interview Electronic Student Survey

Quarter in which appointment occurred: _____

QUIC Interview Company: _____

Rate the level to which the QUIC modules helped inform you about the following:

	Below expectations	Met expectations	Exceeded expectations
QUIC Interview process	☐	☐	☐
How to prepare for your QUIC interview	☐	☐	☐
On-campus interviewing process	☐	☐	☐

How (if at all) could the modules have better met your needs?

_____

Rate the level to which you prepared for the QUIC Interview:
☐ Poor   ☐ Below average   ☐ Average   ☐ Above average   ☐ Excellent

Rate your interviewer on the following:

	Below expectations	Met expectations	Exceeded expectations
Approachability	☐	☐	☐
Clarity of communication	☐	☐	☐
Knowledge of interviewing	☐	☐	☐
Delivery of constructive feedback	☐	☐	☐

How (if at all) could your interviewer have better helped you in the process?

	Below expectations	Met expectations	Exceeded expectations
Rate how well you feel this QUIC interview prepared you for future interviews.	☐	☐	☐

What was the outcome of your QUIC interview?
☐ Passed   ☐ Referral for "More Practice" appointment   ☐ Nonpass

How could this QUIC interview be improved in order to better prepare you?

_____

What is your:
  Specialization _____
  Rank _____
  Gender _____
  Ethnicity _____
  Work authorization _____

Appendix D

Fisher College of Business
Office of Career Management
August 2008 Student Confidence Survey
QUIC Interview Pre- and Postsurvey

Number:_____

Please respond to the following questions and give this sheet to the staff member who will be doing your QUIC interview.

1. **How confident are you about providing specific examples to behavior-based interview questions?**

1	2	3	4
Not at all confident	Somewhat confident	Confident	Very confident

2. **Do you feel confident in your ability to provide evidence of your "fit" with the company?**

1	2	3	4
Not at all confident	Somewhat confident	Confident	Very confident

3. **Are you confident in your ability to "close" the interview?**

1	2	3	4
Not at all confident	Somewhat confident	Confident	Very confident

4. **As of right now, my overall confidence going into the interview is:**

1	2	3	4
Not at all confident	Somewhat confident	Confident	Very confident

Additional Postsurvey Question

Any comments about the part of the QUIC interview that was most helpful to you?

_____

Score:_____

SOUTHERN ILLINOIS UNIVERSITY CARBONDALE

Assessing Career Development Outcomes in a Large Academic Department

Patrick J. Rottinghaus, Meera Komarraju, Julia A. Conrath, and Jane L. Swanson

The Institution

Southern Illinois University Carbondale is a comprehensive public university with an enrollment of approximately 20,000 students (14,000 undergraduates). It is classified by the Carnegie Foundation as a Research University: High Research Activity, the second-highest tier. The undergraduate student body demonstrates considerable racial/ethnic and economic diversity, with many first-generation college students.

Description of the Initiative

Two affiliated programs support students in transition and assess career-related outcomes for the 450 undergraduates in the psychology department: (a) the Career Development and Resource Clinic (CDRC) and (b) a required Careers in Psychology course. The CDRC was established in 2002 to enhance University career counseling services and functions as a training clinic for counseling psychology doctoral students. The Careers in Psychology course was initiated in fall 2008 to enhance students' preparation for successfully entering the job market or securing admission into graduate school.

The CDRC provides career development services, including individual counseling, career assessment, workshops, and presentations to a diverse University community. Counseling services are provided to approximately 100 clients yearly, comprising 40% students of color, 65% women, and 40% graduating students. Although the clientele includes graduate students and community residents, the majority are undergraduates currently exploring academic majors and career options. Many clients are transitioning into the University from two-year institutions and/or are at risk for leaving the institution. Counseling interventions vary in length, typically lasting four to six sessions, and address interests; skills; personality; and values related to selecting a college major (15%), exploring general career directions (60%), or preparing for graduate school (25%). Coordinated with other campus agencies offering academic advising, job placement, and personal counseling, the CDRC services are provided free of charge by doctoral students and supervised by advanced students and faculty. The agency is funded by the psychology department and managed by a faculty member and student coordinator.

As a training clinic in a scientist-practitioner program, the aim is to implement empirically supported interventions into practice. Informed by the growing literature addressing career counseling effectiveness (Oliver & Spokane, 1988; Whiston & Rahardja, 2008), the program emphasizes five critical ingredients that influence the efficacy of career counseling: (a) written exercises, (b) individualized attention, (c) world-of-work information, (d) vicarious learning experiences, and

(e) attention to building support (Brown & Ryan Krane, 2000). All five ingredients can be readily integrated into career assessment interpretations, thereby allowing an opportunity to examine their utility for achieving important career outcomes. Studies examining the effectiveness of career interventions are not only foundational to the literature on career development but provide valuable formative assessment data that can be used to strengthen services offered to students in transition.

In addition to providing career counseling services for managing various career transitions, the second departmental programmatic effort is a course designed to introduce students to the discipline of psychology, improve retention, and facilitate their transition into future educational and occupational opportunities. The Careers in Psychology course was implemented in fall 2008 and is embedded within a larger undergraduate program that includes advisement and various initiatives to enhance student success. This one-credit class is required for all psychology majors and must be completed with a grade of *C* or better. Students are strongly encouraged to complete this course during their first year. The course objectives include (a) learning about interests, skills, and values related to career choice; (b) understanding the degree requirements and course offerings for a psychology major, (c) gaining research and preprofessional practicum experience, (d) acquiring exposure to psychology as a discipline and its subspecialties, (e) identifying career opportunities, (f) applying to graduate school, and (g) becoming familiar with campus resources relevant to educational and professional development (e.g., Writing Center, library, CDRC, Career Services).

These objectives are fulfilled through lectures, small-group discussions, faculty presentations about their research and area of specialization, and panel discussions involving current senior psychology majors and graduate students. The course requirements include contributing to an online discussion, three tests, 10 unannounced in-class quizzes, and eight career-related assignments (i.e., an individualized four-year educational plan, interviewing a professional in the field, career self-exploration, job search, writing a résumé and cover letter, practicing APA style, visiting a research lab and preprofessional site, and a final poster presentation reflecting future career plans).

Research Design

The psychology department's affiliated career-related programs each use numerous outcome measures to evaluate career counseling and academic offerings. In addition to routine counselor and course evaluations, individuals complete validated career assessments (pre- and postintervention) designed to measure change along various dimensions of career development.

To evaluate the effectiveness of career counseling offered in the CDRC, an experimental intervention was instituted in 2006 to examine varying degrees of the five critical ingredients related to career outcomes in a sample of 89 college students. Using interpretations of the Strong Interest Inventory (SII; Donnay, Morris, Schaubhut, & Thompson, 2005) and the Skills Confidence Inventory (SCI; Betz, Borgen, & Harmon, 1996), intervention protocols were carefully documented to enable researchers to monitor the usefulness of various interpretation approaches. The study was comprised of three treatment groups:

- ◇ Group 1: SII group interpretation with no direct attention to the critical ingredients
- ◇ Group 2: SII individual interpretation enhanced with in-session writing and exploration of world-of-work information
- ◇ Group 3: SII and SCI individual interpretation enhanced with attention to vicarious learning experiences and building support

Students who indicated an interest in exploring career concerns were recruited from an introductory undergraduate psychology course. Participants completed a brief demographic and career planning questionnaire, SII, SCI, Career Decision Difficulties Questionnaire (CDDQ; Gati & Saka, 2000), and Career Decision-Making Self-Efficacy – Short Form (CDMSE-SF; Betz & Taylor, 2001) and were then randomly assigned to one of the three groups. After receiving their respective interventions, students immediately completed the Career Planning Questionnaire, CDDQ, and CDMSE-SF again plus a series of quantitative and qualitative questions related to satisfaction with the interpretation and career planning intentions.

A variety of immediate outcomes were examined, including decisional status, career decision-making self-efficacy, and career decision-making difficulties. Larger positive outcomes were expected from the enhanced interventions (Groups 2 and 3) as well as benefits from the group intervention (Group 1).

To evaluate the effectiveness of the Careers in Psychology course and explore any course changes, data from 79 students were obtained from an analysis of posts to an online discussion question, course evaluations, and a pretest-posttest design administered at the beginning and end of two semesters (i.e., fall 2008 and spring 2009). The pretest and posttest included the CDMSE-SF (Betz & Taylor, 2001), comprising five subscales relating to career choice competencies (i.e., making accurate self-appraisals, obtaining occupational information, selecting goals, planning for the future, and solving problems); the 28-item Academic Motivation Scale (Vallerand et al.,1992), comprising three subscales (i.e., intrinsic, extrinsic, and amotivation); and an in-house scale developed to measure attitudes towards the psychology major. These specific measures were selected as the course is designed to increase career self-efficacy and to explore whether increased self-efficacy is associated with increased motivation (intrinsic and extrinsic).

Findings

CDRC Critical Ingredients Intervention Study

Using a paired samples t-test, the overall CDDQ scores decreased over time, $t(87) = 2.55$, $p < .05$. This demonstrated that interventions were effective generally. A repeated measures MANOVA using the three CDDQ and the five CDMSE scales as dependent measures found no significant effects for Time, or Time X Group interaction. Although no significant multivariate treatment effects were found, possibly due to limited power, there was a significant Time X Group interaction for Occupational Information Self-Efficacy, $F(2, 84) = 4.77, p < .05, \eta^2 = .102$. As shown in Figure 1, participants who received individualized attention showed gains, especially for Group 2, which received enhanced attention to exploring career information, whereas Group 1 decreased on this subscale. This result highlights a specific outcome related to the actual activities incorporated within the intervention. Overall, these results demonstrated that attending to the five critical ingredients contributes to meaningful outcomes of career assessment interpretations.

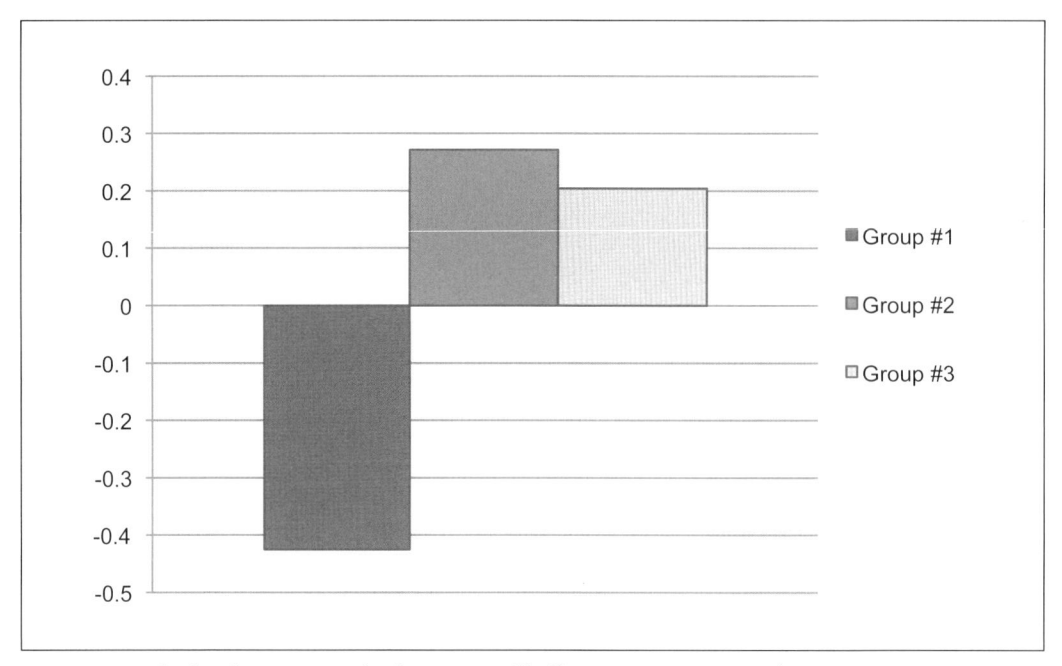

Figure 1. Standardized occupational information self-efficacy Time 2-Time 1 change scores.

Careers in Psychology Course

Analysis of the posts to the online class discussion question as well as the end of semester course evaluations indicated that students found this new course to be beneficial in helping them think about various career possibilities and alerting them to resources that could be used in enhancing their professional development. Junior- and senior-level students who took the course, although it was not required for them, stated that it would have been helpful if this course had been offered during their first or sophomore year as they could have made more thoughtful choices and consciously pursued research and internship opportunities. Paired samples t-tests indicated there were significant differences between pretest and posttest responses on the career self-efficacy subscales. These results suggest that the course improved students' knowledge about careers in psychology; enhanced the accuracy of their self-appraisal; increased their knowledge of occupational information; and helped in selecting career goals, planning for the future, and solving problems related to progress in their careers (Komarraju, Swanson, & Tincher, 2010). A calculation of Cohen's *d*, to test the significance of mean differences, revealed effect sizes ranging from moderate to large. Further, there was a significant positive correlation between the various subscales of career self-efficacy and both types of academic motivation (i.e., intrinsic and extrinsic). These correlations ranged from .24 to .42, with stronger correlations between the self-efficacy subscales and intrinsic motivation (.32 to .42) than between self-efficacy subscales and extrinsic motivation (.24 to .29).

Conclusion

These two programs each incorporate activities informed by relevant literature and demonstrate the effectiveness of the five critical ingredients of career counseling (Brown & Ryan Krane, 2000) and factors involved in student retention and engagement (Kuh, 2001). Through reflection on ongoing efforts, recommendations are offered for strategically evaluating career services for students within broad disciplines (e.g., psychology) that translate into diverse career opportunities. These experiences have provided insights into the challenges of conducting action research while offering an opportunity to consider how the CDRC and Careers in Psychology course complement one another.

Although the CDRC experiment had limited duration and power, results support the practice of attending to the identified critical ingredients of career counseling and the potential for enhancing the consequential validity of career assessments and interpretations. This study represents an early attempt to examine these factors locally; however, notable shortcomings include that the interventions involved a limited duration of two sessions and did not involve actual clients. Future research will extend this work by recruiting actual CDRC clients presenting with career undecidedness. This strategy more closely follows the advice of others conducting career outcomes research by recruiting actual clients (Swanson, 1995).

Overall outcomes research on current CDRC clients is ongoing. Admittedly, establishing and implementing a strategic evaluation system is difficult and requires careful attention from all staff. A model program would involve continuing efforts to identify standard measures of specific programmatic objectives and include mechanisms for conducting follow-up surveys immediately upon the conclusion of counseling and periodically thereafter. Obtaining follow-up data is inherently challenging, the department is making great progress in establishing a system to collect pre-post outcomes on these dimensions. All CDRC clients now complete the Career Futures Inventory-Revised (CFI-R; Rottinghaus, 2007) at intake and termination. The CFI-R measures the following dimensions of career adaptability: self-awareness, occupational awareness, career optimism, control, support, career transition confidence, and work-life balance. Moreover, individualized application of the five critical ingredients can likely be strengthened within the context of a carefully coordinated local system (e.g., connecting CDRC resources with local occupational information and resources through academic and other programmatic offerings).

The Careers in Psychology course affords a unique opportunity to help students explore realistic linkages between the discipline of psychology and meaningful career possibilities. In an effort to improve the delivery and quality of the course as well as the undergraduate program, the following changes have been implemented while continuing to evaluate and revise the course:

- A second advisor has been added to serve as a teaching assistant for the course and handle the increased demand for advisement appointments.
- The number of faculty presentations has been increased to cover a wider range of subspecialties.
- To build community and a sense of continuity, faculty presentations and panel discussions are introduced only after the first three weeks of the semester.
- A new attendance policy has been adopted to address student attendance concerns (i.e., about 10-15% do not attend regularly and miss submitting the career-related assignments). Students who miss class or fail to submit assignments are also sent e-mails reminding them of absences and providing details regarding upcoming assignments. In addition, it is now mandatory for students to complete all career-related assignments for partial credit even if they miss the initial deadlines.

For the future, a recommendation is to change the course format to include small breakout discussion sections. Course enrollment has been increasing from the first offering with about 60 students to 139, but this large lecture setting reduces opportunities for student/faculty interaction and personalized performance feedback. Since this is an important element of student success, the possibility of increasing the number of credits from one to three is being explored to allow for two lectures and one day for small breakout sessions of 25-30 students. It is anticipated this will allow coverage of a wider range of topics in greater depth and give students an opportunity to know their peers and engage in a larger number of career-related activities designed to enhance career self-efficacy.

Taken together, these related programs provide multimodal opportunities for helping transitioning students with the challenging task of identifying career options within a broad field such as psychology. Large academic departments have an additional burden of engaging a number of diverse students with a variety of needs and desires regarding career assistance. However, such large departments frequently have additional resources to address diverse students' needs and may be able to draw upon resources from other institutional units outside the department. The programs mentioned herein enable the University's psychology department to meet regularly with its students, particularly in their first year, allowing enhanced orientation to the discipline and provide counseling services to support the exploration of career possibilities.

An ongoing review of evaluation systems can optimize efforts to identify critical needs of students as well as effectiveness of programs. In addition to simply assessing outcomes, it is recommended that administrators, faculty, and career development professionals explore ways that local results can inform ongoing practice, training, and development activities. In addition to individual counseling interventions, methods to unite efforts from the CDRC program with additional student development efforts within the psychology department and other student development agencies across the University are being explored.

References

Betz, N. E., Borgen, F. H., & Harmon, L. W. (1996). *Skills Confidence Inventory.* Palo Alto, CA: Consulting Psychologists Press.

Betz, N. E., & Taylor, K. M. (2001). *Manual for the Career Decision Self-Efficacy Scale and CDMSE - Short Form.* Columbus, OH: The Ohio State University.

Brown, S. D., & Ryan Krane, N. E. (2000). Four (or five) sessions and a cloud of dust: Old assumptions and new observations about career counseling. In S. D. Brown & R. W. Lent (Eds.), *Handbook of counseling psychology* (3rd ed., pp. 740-766). New York, NY: Wiley.

Donnay, D. A. C., Morris, M. A., Schaubhut, N. A., & Thompson, R. C. (2005). *Strong Interest Inventory manual: Research, development, and strategies for interpretation.* Palo Alto, CA: Consulting Psychologists Press.

Gati, I., & Saka, N. (2000). Internet-based versus paper-and-pencil assessment: Measuring career decision-making difficulties. *Journal of Career Assessment, 9,* 397-416.

Komarraju, M., Swanson, J., & Tincher, C. (2010, January). *A course to increase psychology majors' career self-efficacy.* Poster session presented at the National Institute on the Teaching of Psychology Conference, St. Petersburg, FL.

Kuh, G. D. (2001, May/June). Assessing what really matters to student learning: Inside the National Survey of Student Engagement. *Change, 33*(3), 10-17, 66.

Oliver, L. W., & Spokane, A. R. (1988). Career-intervention outcome: What contributes to client gain? *Journal of Counseling Psychology, 35,* 447-462.

Rottinghaus, P. J. (2007). *Career Futures Inventory - Revised.* Carbondale, IL: Author.

Swanson, J. L. (1995). The process and outcome of career counseling. In W. B. Walsh & S. H. Osipow (Eds.), *Handbook of vocational psychology* (2nd ed., pp. 217-259). Mahwah, NJ: Lawrence Erlbaum Associates.

Vallerand, R. J., Pelletier, L. G., Blais, M. R., Briere, N. M., Senecal, C., & Vallieres, E. F. (1992). The Academic Motivation Scale: A measure of intrinsic, extrinsic, and amotivation in education. *Educational and Psychological Measurement, 52,* 1003-1017.

Whiston, S. C., & Rahardia, D. (2008). Vocational counseling process and outcome. In S. D. Brown & R. W. Lent (Eds.), *Handbook of counseling psychology* (4th ed., pp. 444-461). Hoboken, NJ: Wiley.

About the Chapter Authors

LOUISA P. CARTER is pursuing a doctoral degree in counseling psychology in the Department of Educational Psychology at the University of Utah with a research interest in first-generation college students. She has spent three years as a research assistant for the Retention and Assessment Committee at the University of Utah, providing support in various school-wide initiatives. Carter has also been involved in research projects to develop and deliver a high school based student success program and has aided in building a student success inventory for a comprehensive student success model.

BENGÜ ERGÜNER-TEKINALP is an assistant professor in the Counselor Education program at Drake University in Des Moines, Iowa. She received her doctoral degree in counselor education from Auburn University in Alabama. Her research interests are multicultural counseling, social justice, and advocacy. Ergüner-Tekinalp has conducted research on school counselor roles and school counseling program effectiveness, as well as a cross cultural investigation of eating disorders. She and her colleagues adapted the Emotional Abuse Questionnaire to Turkish.

PAUL A. GORE, JR. is an associate professor and student success special projects coordinator at the University of Utah. In addition to his academic and student support roles, Gore serves as the director of institutional analysis. He holds a PhD in counseling psychology from Loyola University – Chicago, and master's degrees in counseling and applied biopsychology. Prior to arriving in Utah, Gore served as the director of the Career Transitions Research Department at ACT, Inc. in Iowa City, where he helped develop instruments, programs, and services in support of students' academic and career transitions. He has authored more than 40 peer-reviewed journal articles and book chapters and was editor of the National Resource Center for The First Year Experience and Students in Transition (NRC) monograph, *Facilitating the Career Development of Students in Transition*. He is the past-chair of the Society for Vocational Psychology and currently is an NRC advisory board member. Gore also serves on the editorial boards of several journals that focus on higher education, student development, and vocational psychology.

BRIANA K. KELLER earned her PhD in counseling psychology from Indiana University. Keller is the assistant director of the Career Center at the University of Washington in Seattle where she coordinates the Center's programming for graduate students, provides individual counseling for students and alumni in a wide range of disciplines, facilitates workshops and events, comanages the Center's marketing efforts, and helps track and analyze students' usage of the Center's services.

WADE C. LEUWERKE is currently an associate professor in the Counselor Education program at Drake University in Des Moines, Iowa. He earned a PhD in counseling psychology from Southern Illinois University Carbondale. His research and professional activities have examined factors that predict college major retention, the impact of computer-assisted career guidance systems on academic planning and career exploration behaviors, and the role of technology in career development processes. He has experience examining school counselors' roles and working with professional school counselors to positively impact students' academic development, career and college exploration, and the acquisition of personal and social skills that will prepare them for college and life beyond.

RACHEL F. PICKETT is an assistant professor of psychology at Concordia University Wisconsin. She received her PhD in counseling psychology from Southern Illinois University Carbondale. Pickett teaches clinical and research courses and supervises senior students' practicum and research projects. She also teaches a first-year experience course. Her research examines topics in college student development, vocational psychology, and multicultural issues.